Advance praise for
COMPETE AND EMPOWER

"I think a lot of people get involved in politics without a firm understanding of what really drives the economy, which is the private sector, and I think it's important for politicians to have that understanding... It (Compete and Empower) shares exactly the type of philosophy that would get people back to work and actually increase tax receipts at a time when we're pretty much in a recession."

**—Ty Cobb (R) Nevada Assemblyman and Candidate,
State Senate District 4 (Washoe, Nevada)**

"This book is based on the history of what every successful corporation has been doing for 30 years. I believe it is a very good, well thought out approach for anyone who wants the country to solve the problems we are facing today."

**—Jerry Harrison, retired, CEO of the engineering firm
Stearns-Roger World Corporation during the 1980s**

"I have found Mr. Sear's *Compete and Empower* well thought out and factually supported. It is timely, the message is clear and we must act now if America is to compete with other developing nations of the world, such as China."

**—Bill Nicholson, vice president and senior executive at both
public and private companies in Silicon Valley, California**

"Brian Sear's book is a great recipe for capitalism, and a great plan for the country. *Compete and Empower* fulfills our founding fathers' vision of a free society that can compete in trade on an equal and a moral plane with the other countries of the world. It is the way the country should go."

—Roger Block, founder of a high-tech company in Minden, Nevada, and owner of Thunder Canyon Country Club in Washoe Valley, Nevada.

COMPETE
AND
EMPOWER

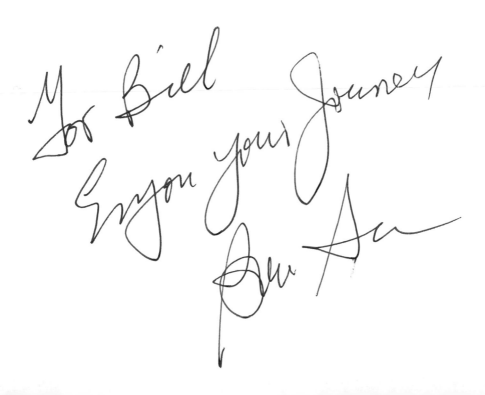

For Bill
Enjoy your Journey

COMPETE
AND
EMPOWER
INCREASING WEALTH
FOSTERING FREEDOM

BEAVER'S
POND
PRESS

BRIAN SEAR

ISBN 10: 1-59298-306-5
ISBN 13: 978-159298-306-3

Library of Congress Catalog Number: 2009941378

Printed in the United States of America

First Printing: 2010

14 13 12 11 10   5 4 3 2 1

Cover and interior design by James Monroe Design, LLC.

Beaver's Pond Press, Inc.
7104 Ohms Lane, Suite 101
Edina, MN 55439-2129
(952) 829-8818
www.BeaversPondPress.com

To order, visit www.BeaversPondBooks.com
or call (800) 901-3480. Reseller discounts available.

Dedicated to
MERLE
My late wife, a lovely lady, and the love of my life for thirty-eight years
and to
MARK and STEPHEN
Our two sons, who make me proud.

CONTENTS

PREFACE

People in this country are frustrated. Our government keeps getting bigger and bigger. Politicians aren't listening to the people. As a world leader, America seems to be falling farther and farther behind. Even our experts predict China will soon overtake the United States as a world leader. Peace seems impossible across the globe.

What has gone wrong? Is there anything a concerned American citizen can do?

Yes, there is. First, we can place our trust in the U.S. Constitution, an incredible gift to mankind. In their hearts and souls, our Founding Fathers held a deep-seated belief that virtuous people living in liberty and freedom, and guided by a framework of natural laws, would provide fairness and justice for all. Furthermore they believed that citizen public servants, working for the people, would allow free markets and capitalism to flourish and provide prosperity and peace for everyone.

Second, we can learn from Bruce Henderson's Boston Consulting Group (BCG) unique perspectives on natural competition, which he developed in the 1960s to lead businesses to success. He proved that when businesses are allowed to compete freely, natural competition leads to peace and stability, something we all hunger for.

We can—and will—get this country back on track if we do two things:

1. Actually follow the Constitution, and

2. Apply the principles of natural business competition to running our government.

That's what this book is about. It will explain the damage caused by the doctrine used for thousands of years by people in power, which I call Conquer and Oppress, a doctrine that has led only to tragic cycles of human deprivation and destruction. Conquer and Oppress is an unstable doctrine that cannot empower great societies or world order.

Using the American Constitution, the principles of natural competition, and years of experience working with growing companies, I've developed a new doctrine that I call *Compete and Empower*.

As I've created strategic tools to help young companies grow and prosper, it became clear that *Compete and Empower*, based on the natural laws of competition and supported by the principles of the Constitution, could be a more effective model for governments to follow instead of Conquer and Oppress.

I wrote this book to lay a foundation we can all use to better understand the contribution that the Constitution made to the growth of world wealth from 1800 and the contribution that natural competition played in even faster growth from 1960 on. The principles discussed show us a better path for our government to take.

The United States of America is the greatest democracy in the history of this planet. If, we, the people, can build a government willing to replace Conquer and Oppress with *Compete and Empower*, America's greatness will never dim. *Compete and Empower* is about achieving that dream.

CHAPTER**ONE**

CIVILIZATION

We can make the world a better place for all the people

From the Stone Age to the Secular Age, human beings as individuals have adapted to the world around them with incredible alacrity. Homo Sapiens-Sapiens are self-reliant spiritual people that have survived, evolved, developed, invented, produced, and contributed so much wealth to all mankind. Unfortunately throughout recorded history man has not created and developed successful virtuous societies that have weathered the passage of time. The overriding reason for failing as architects of civilization is that the privileged few, who are granted by the people to lead the societies, have turned to a doctrine of Conquer and Oppress to control the people.

Prosperity for all the peoples of our world can be achieved peacefully by adopting new perspectives on competition between businesses and nations. This book is a wake-up call for

America's leaders in government, corporations, and the media, and a call to action for U.S. citizens.

In this book I will present the story of what works. This is a pragmatic approach that may appear to favor one ideology over another, but instead reveals historical facts showing which ideas have failed and which have produced positive results. The solutions that will work require substantial change to solve the American challenge in the twenty-first century. I hope you will enjoy this new perspective and join with me to successfully forge the American dream.

How will this happen? We will replace Conquer and Oppress, the brutal conquering methods used throughout human history, with free trade and capitalism. This book is a road map through human history and survival and a strategic planning guide that will show you a better path to a civilized future using the *Compete and Empower* philosophy.

People and the businesses they grow, with a helping hand from the societies they create, are the only source of prosperity for developing a virtuous, just, and peaceful world. The natural way, our Creator's way, is to call on human beings to first survive and then to lead a purpose-driven life. In order to achieve this, people need a physical environment that is conducive to survival and a society in which they have an unalienable right to life, liberty, and the pursuit of happiness.

Although we have failed to organize our civilization in a successful and virtuous way, we have been given two gifts of great potential that can transform our world to a utopia we can all be proud of. They are: *The American Constitution* by the Founding Fathers and the *Perspectives on Natural Competition* by Bruce Henderson. Let us briefly review history and the current situation to prepare us for the changes we must make in order to create a virtuous world in balance with nature and human aspirations.

THE MALTHUSIAN TRAP OR POVERTY TRAP

According to Gregory Clark, in his book titled *A Farewell to Alms, a brief economic history of the world*, our progress as civilized societies has two distinct periods. The poverty, or Malthusian, trap ran from recorded history 7,000 years ago to 1800 and the industrial revolution from 1800 to the mid-twentieth century. Clark also describes the period from 1800 on as a period of divergence. For the first time the wealth of the common man started to increase at a world average of about 0.9 percent per year. Unfortunately this benefit, borne of individual inventions, did not accrue evenly across all nations. Britain initiated the breakthrough. Then increasing wealth per person quickly emerged in several western nations including the United States.

Adding to Clark's research and premises, I discovered that another period from 1960 to present time is important to clarify. This was the information age, driven by computer and communication technology that enabled world gross domestic product (GDP) to grow about 5 percent per year.

THREE PERIODS OF WEALTH DEVELOPMENT

Clark discusses several causes and effects that resulted in no wealth improvement of the average person for 7,000 years, and a divergence in wealth between nations from 1800. According to Clark, until 1800 the life of the common man did not improve much, if any, over his Stone Age ancestor.

Three Periods of World Wealth

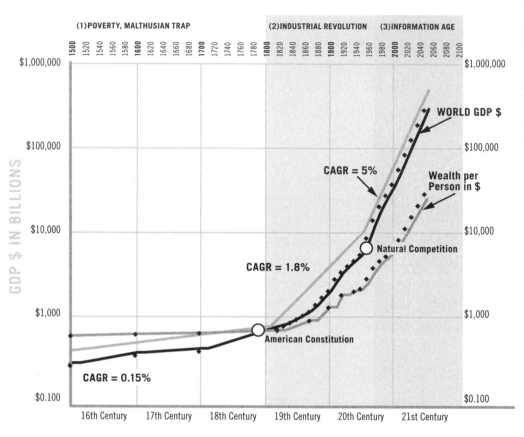

During this period there were many different societies, with various attributes and inventions with the potential to improve prosperity for all the people. Poverty was not overcome because the population increased and the wealth accumulated only in the pockets of a few elites who controlled the population economically. Population, a function of birth and death rates, was also controlled by the environment. Populations may increase rapidly for a few generations and then be cut back by war, famine, or disease.

This was called the Malthusian Trap because of the theories written about by Thomas Malthus in his book titled *Essay of the Principles of Population*, published in 1798.

THE INDUSTRIAL REVOLUTION

The industrial boost to average wealth started in England with a confluence of inventions in technology (steam engines, electricity, etc.), readily available energy (coal), a reduction in birthrate, and an improvement in society institutions (more democratic). The combination of these factors, along with similar circumstances in a few western nations, caused world GDP to rise at about 1.8 percent.

The wealth of all the people wasn't increased dramatically because the elites were still in control even though the improved societies were governed somewhat more democratically. However the wealth of the average citizen did increase at about 0.9 percent, which was better than the Malthusian trap period. In the early twentieth century, progress was further hindered by many nations experimenting with the collectivist theories of Karl Marx. By following communism and socialism, these societies violated the natural need for man to be free to pursue life, liberty, and the pursuit of happiness.

Although some would argue that the cause of this improvement in wealth was the inventions and technology of the Nineteenth century, I believe the contribution by America's Constitution freeing the citizens to grow the GDP faster than any other nation was significant.

THE INFORMATION AGE

From 1960 to today, there has been an explosion of innovation, invention, technology, and entrepreneurship. In fifty short years semiconductors have enabled a powerful computer to fit in the palm of your hand. Wireless technology has enabled communication from person to person around the world. Fiber optics has provided a way to transfer enormous amounts of data at lightning speed so that we can share pictures and teleconference from country to country.

Because productivity has increased and knowledge has spread, world GDP has grown at 5 percent. Wealth is being shared with more and more people but there is still a significant divergence between nations and between the citizens of these nations. During this period average wealth grew at about 2.6 percent per year.

Although the technology inventions and developments contributed greatly to this growth rate, I discovered that understanding natural and business competition transformed many modern corporations into organizations that competed effectively, grew rapidly, moved down the experience curve, and satisfied customers.

THE GREAT DIVERGENCE

Today Planet Earth is home to about two hundred nations and 6.8 billion people. One hundred and thirty nine nations out of One hundred and ninety two—about 72 percent—govern in such a way that their citizens subsist on less than $10,000 per person. This is considered below the poverty level for a civilized society. These 139 nations are home to about 5.5 billion people. This means about 81 percent of all the people on earth are attempting to survive on less than $10,000 per person per year. Even worse, about 2.5 billion people (38 percent) suffer on $1,000 per year.

Not only is there this devastating divergence on poverty but the divergence of GDP per nation is also significant, because one nation, America, has become over three times larger than any other nation. It must be doing something quite profound to have achieved so much in so little time.

In 2008 American business produced over $14 trillion in GDP, which is over three times larger than its nearest competitors China and Japan, each at about $4 trillion. America's impact on the world economy is enormous because of its size and strength. If only our political leaders realized this and stopped tinkering with minor issues that have often resulted in unintended consequences around the globe.

Clark expressed his opinion that the Malthusian Trap and the performance since 1800 is the result of many natural factors affecting the human experience. The causes are complex and therefore difficult to overcome. Although I agree in general with Clark, I believe a primary driving force dominates all other variables. Throughout recorded history, as individuals have taken control or been elected to lead nations, these leaders have used their power to Conquer and Oppress the people. As a result several thousand elites, so called-leaders, have caused the suffering and misery of many of the planet's 6.8 billion people.

Conquer and Oppress can take many forms. Some are obvious such as revolutionaries, dictators, communist, and socialist governments, fascism, imperialism, and colonialism. Even America, with its Constitution providing freedom and liberty, has been slowly but surely taken over by its government over the last one hundred years. Citizen politicians, enjoying the power of the office, became career politicians and have started to oppress the people with excessive laws, regulation, and taxation.

Our leaders have failed to empower the inherent talents of the people, and this pitiful performance has got to stop. Clearly there have been exceptions in leadership throughout history, yet our experiments with civilization have led to 5.5 billion people out of 6.8 billion living below the poverty line. In the last one hundred years alone there have been seventy wars, tens of millions of people killed or slaughtered, and millions starved to death.

Many will say there is plenty of blame to go around, but if we are honest with ourselves, we know that the only people ultimately accountable for this dysfunctional world are the leaders who savored power, put themselves in charge, and abused power over the people.

TWO MIRACLES THAT PROVIDE A FUTURE WORTH STRIVING FOR

The first miracle occurred at the beginning of the industrial revolution and at the start of improving productivity and wealth per person, when our Founding Fathers wrote the American Constitution. The United States, a new nation under God, had just begun. By July 4, 1776, America adopted the Declaration of Independence from Britain. In 230 years America has gone from a standing start to the finest democracy the world has ever known.

America provides outstanding technology, products, and services around the world with about 28 percent market share of world GDP. Its nearest competitors have less than 10 percent. We have the most powerful and technically advanced military, we have freedoms that other nations would die for, and we are very charitable. There must be something special about America to have come so far so quickly and there is. It's called the Constitution!

The Constitution provides the liberty and freedom for citizens to pursue their dreams and because the people have virtue, character, and courage and believe in free market capitalism the citizen's dreams can come true. This dynamic combination enabled America to grow faster and better than any other nation in spite of the lack of leadership from career politicians. Think how well we could have done and what an example we could have been to the rest of the world if our leaders had kept their oath to follow the Constitution and remain public servants instead of career politicians. Currently their interests in feathering their own nests directly conflicts with the expectations of the people. For America to be the best it can be, and lead the world to prosperity and peace, this situation must change. Not convinced? Read W. Cleon Skousen's *The 5000 Year Leap. A Miracle that Changed the World*!

Cleon Skousen during many years of research, reading, and sharing with others about the importance of the Constitution discovered that all the legalese could be boiled down to twenty eight very important principles. A major portion of his book is devoted to these principles, which he discusses in easy-to-comprehend prose. Because I believe in these principles and believe that our leaders lost sight of many of our Constitution's principles over the last one hundred years to the people's and country's detriment, I hope the reader will return to our roots and realize how important the twenty eight principles are to our future.

The second miracle occurred in the 1960s. While the beginning of the information age increased productivity, the real impetus for American success was new perspectives on natural and strategic competition developed by Bruce Henderson of BCG.

Henderson's ideas transformed American business into strategic enterprises that learned how to succeed in market segments and get a good return on investment (ROI).

Those companies that stayed stuck in the robber baron days, with an operating philosophy of management versus the workers, failed to take advantage of these new strategies. They succumbed to union demands, lost market share, became unprofitable, and went out of business.

From my early work developing strategy and tools for young companies I developed the theory that using *Compete and Empower* in market segments was the best doctrine for succeeding in business. American businesses that embraced a strategic plan based on these principles became the driving force for our superior growth in the last fifty years. The exciting thing is that these principles can be applied to more than business. They can be used to develop entire nations.

In order to do this we must explore the major elements: people, prosperity, polarization, natural competition, business competition, and a road to peace. Built in sequence, these subjects will lead you to a plan, action, and results for America.

We need courageous change to lead the world to prosperity and peace in the twenty-first century and our citizens have that courage.

Let's move on to a discussion about people and what drives them, since empowering the people is what it's all about.

CHAPTER**TWO**

PEOPLE

Empowering the People is what it's all about

From the beginning, human beings embarked on a tough and tortuous journey with a hint of joy and discovery. Unfortunately the journey was also peppered with periods of tyranny and terror. To empower the people of today to create a prosperous, peaceful world in harmony with our environment, it is helpful to revisit history and understand the natural laws of human evolution and motivation.

A BRIEF HISTORY OF MAN'S SURVIVAL

About one hundred thousand years ago early man, Homo Sapiens-Sapiens, was a hunter, warrior, gatherer with tribal instincts. Survival required instinctive self-reliance and a learned skill to cooperate with family and neighbors. The male was usually the hunter and warrior, and the female became a gatherer and took care of the children. As they became mature, the children participated in survival activities within the family first and then the tribe.

Initially survival required hard work from dawn to dusk. Survival of the fittest became the natural behavior as humans learned to grow and to survive in an environment that was always changing. Environmental change occurred from season to season, from year to year with significant affect on their ability to provide adequate food, shelter, and clothing. It was a tough and difficult life.

As time passed man learned how to satisfy his basic needs of survival, and eventually man found time in the day to use this excess for purposes beyond survival. Some chose to improve their lot with newfound wealth from tools, products, or services and barter with others. Some may have chosen to relax and participate in activities that were enjoyable but not wealth generating. Over time some would become wealthier and more powerful than others. As long as each member of the family and tribe respected other members, and accepted each individual's freedom to choose their own journey, then life was peaceful but still tough and harsh.

It's possible that such behavior could lead to utopian societies. In some cases it did. Consider a quote from *A People's History of the USA* by Howard Zinn, from the log of Christopher Columbus when he arrived in the Bahamas and met Arawak Indians.

"They … brought us parrots and balls of cotton and spears
and many other things, which they exchanged for
the glass beads and hawks' bells.

They willingly traded everything they owned ...
They were well built, with good bodies
and handsome features ... They do not bear arms, and do
not know them, for I showed them a sword, they took it by
an edge and cut themselves out of ignorance.
They have no iron. Their spears are made of cane ...
They would make fine servants ...
With fifty men we could subjugate them all
and make them do whatever we want."

Clearly the Arawak Indians had evolved into a society that treated its people with respect. Unfortunately, as suggested by Columbus's log, not everyone practiced this behavior. A few developed a deviant, sinful behavior. After becoming more wealthy and powerful, these bullies or deviant individuals looked down upon their fellow partners in the tribe and took control, either by coercing or killing dissenters. Once in power these questionable leaders, some may call dictators, set up onerous conditions to control the workers or slaves. So began the principle of the two-class system: The elites versus the underclass.

Clearly Columbus, a great explorer and a fine man, did not respect the Arawak Indians and the peaceful society they had developed. He was more interested in achieving the goals of his mission, than learning the attributes of the Arawak Indian society. Therefore he considered how easy it would be to conquer and enslave them. Somewhere in the western European experience, this reputable explorer picked up an abhorrent behavior that provided him a short term gain at the long term expense of a better society.

I call this doctrine of government Conquer and Oppress and believe it is the primary reason why 5.5 billion of the world's 6.8 billion population live in poverty. Today the governments of all the two hundred nations still exercise the Conquer and Oppress doctrine in one form or another over their citizens.

We have seen societies come and go. Phoenician, Greek, Roman, Ottoman, Dane, Portuguese, Spanish, Chinese, Japanese, Russian, and British were all successful societies for a while but they eventually failed. They tried monarchies, imperialism, colonialism communism, and socialism—all interesting theories—but when elites conquered and oppressed the citizens, those societies diminished.

Even America, with its Constitution calling for freedom and liberty for all the people, has been hijacked by career politicians who erode liberty and burden the people with excessive laws, regulations, and taxes.

SELF-RELIANCE IS A VIRTUE

In 1776 Thomas Jefferson wrote, in the opening of the Declaration of Independence, the following:

> *"We hold these truths to be self-evident, that all men*
> *are created equal, that they are endowed by their Creator*
> *with certain unalienable Rights, that among these are*
> *Life, Liberty, and the Pursuit of Happiness."*

I quote this here because it is important to understand that man is created with equal rights, not necessarily with equal genes. The progress or success man makes for himself in his lifetime is the result of both genes and experience. Just because our Creator gave us equal rights does not guarantee equal outcomes. Living life to the fullest is risky business. If you could ask one of our early ancestors about Stone Age life you would find out just how risky.

Man instinctively chose to learn, grow, and change as the best way to survive over time. Because, throughout history, man has had to cope with both natural and man-made disasters, man has evolved to be self-reliant, finding this to be the best course for a purpose-driven life.

Government elites with power over the people cannot provide high productivity, wealth, and prosperity for all the people because their methods directly conflict with human nature. If leaders convince the people they are inferior, victims, working class, underdogs, not worthy of the good things in life, then those people become unproductive, unfulfilled, and dependent. On the other hand, if parents and community and society leaders communicate to the children that they must learn, grow, and change every day, then we will develop a prosperous and peaceful world.

It is a fundamental truth that each person can achieve any goal no matter how difficult it may seem, providing the person is willing to learn, grow, and change every day. This is true no matter how humble the beginnings or how lacking in initial capabilities.

After leaving high school at seventeen years of age I went to work for Shell Petroleum in London. Prior to being conscripted into the Royal Air Force (RAF) in June 1954 Shell Petroleum gave me the opportunity in March 1954 to attend "Outward Bound Mountain School" at Eskdale Green, located in the Lake District, UK for a thirty-day course. Outward Bound was started in England during World War II to encourage young military personnel to fight for survival no matter how difficult the circumstances. In addition to the Outward Bound Mountain School they opened a Sea School in Aberdovey, Wales.

In the March 1954 class about ninety students from all walks of life were brought together to be tested by harsh conditions. Toward the end we were broken up into eight groups and sent out on the mountain for three days to survive in snow and ice and scale two mountain peaks. You can see our group pictured below. I am in the center of the lower row.

The brilliance of the school's curriculum is that, it was not just about survival, but it was also about the growth and learning experience of each individual. The school's highest honor did not go to the most capable when the person arrived for the thirty-day training, but to the individual who made the most progress from his starting point. The highest honor for personal progress was called an Honor Medal for excellent performance. The runner-up award was called a Merit Medal for outstanding growth in thirty days. The participation award was called the Membership Medal and was given to each person who had stayed the course, had shown potential to grow, and had survived. In my class of ninety about 2 percent dropped out, 10 percent got Merit Medals, and not one person was awarded the Honor Medal. The Honor Medal was very difficult to achieve because it required changing within thirty days to a new philosophy with significant progress. I was fortunate to receive a Merit Medal, but more importantly this simple principle of being willing to learn, grow, and change altered my life and attitude forever.

How I wish our schools today taught this fundamental principle of life. It is in our genes, instinctively part of our survival mechanism, but needs to be encouraged and supported by parents, educators, and mentors.

Over my lifetime I have found that in order to pursue a productive, prosperous, purpose-driven life it helps to follow certain principles. These seven basic principles have worked for me and those I have mentored as we pursued our dreams.

Basic Principles for Personal Growth:

1. **Accept that all men are created equal ...** A constitution should grant equal rights but not guarantee equal outcomes.

2. **Do unto others as you would do unto yourself ...** Treat people with respect. Accept their choices in life even if they differ from yours.

3. **Recognize that the human experience is almost infinite ...** Improvements in personal performance are possible over a wide dynamic range if one works at learning, growing, and improving every day. Focus on growth in spiritual awareness, knowledge accumulation or physical attributes that fit your passion and are valued in the society of your choice.

4. **Choose your commitments carefully ...** Realize that a person is only as good as his word. Keep all

commitments, and consider that they can only be changed by mutual agreement. Remember that what goes around comes around. The person you blow off today may be in a position to affect you in the future.

5. **Accept change as the only constant in a successful life ...** We find ourselves in environments that may be unpredictable and full of risk. Be willing to change if your needs aren't met. Be prepared to turn over many rocks until you find a nugget. Do not become a victim expecting a handout. Earn success by showing a willingness to support yourself and your family.

6. **Practice egoism by being responsible in your society ...** Act rationally in your own and your family's self-interest, and share your experience with others if they show a willingness to learn. Remember the parable of the fisherman who said, "if you give a person a fish, you feed him for a day. If you teach a person how to fish, you feed him for a lifetime."

7. **Practice altruism only with your own time and money ...** If a person decides it's in his own self-interest to practice altruism, then he should do so with his own time and assets. Do not be altruistic with other people's money, as a politician does when he confiscates wealth from some through taxation to give to others to garner votes. A good example of appropriate altruism is Bill Gates, who made a fortune as an entrepreneur and now spends his time applying venture capital principles to philanthropic endeavors of his own choice with his own money.

Ayn Rand in her book *Atlas Shrugged* said it best when she wrote that egoism is a better philosophy than altruism to develop the heart of a civilization. Unfortunately she tried to be too cute in early promotion of her books by saying, "Egoism is the virtue of Selfishness" instead of using self-reliance. Detractors jumped on this and made it more difficult to spread the word of the importance of her ground-breaking work. Our current leaders need to revisit Ayn's work on the benefits of self-reliance and a strong work ethic. In addition, they need to embrace egoism and the principals of our Founding Fathers that are found within Ayn Rand's philosophy.

Even Alan Greenspan, a man who participated in Ayn Rand creative sessions, appears to have bowed to political correctness. In his latest book, *The Age of Turbulence*, he suggests that there is a struggle between man's desire to increase material wealth and the desire to ward off change and its attendant stress. There is a struggle between entrepreneurship, competitive creative destruction, and protection, job security, and stress reduction. He is implying that it is acceptable for a human being designed to survive to become dependent on the government for one's security. Even if his thesis has merit, we must lead our people to self-reliance and willingness to learn, grow, and change. Great leadership can show the way to prosperity and peace by embracing egoism and entrepreneurship and in doing so help our fellow man to overcome insecurity and stress.

POPULATION OBSERVATIONS

Population estimates for the planet during the Malthusian Trap period to about 1500 ranged from 50,000 to 400,000. These estimates are speculative because of lack of data and are quite variable from time to time as societies changed. Angus Maddison in his book *Contours of the World Economy 1-2030 AD* provides one of the best insights into historical data. Population may have risen rapidly in times of peace and high birth rates and plummeted during periods of war, disease, and famine. After 1700 world population exploded from about 500,000 people to over 6 billion in 2000. Improvements in hygiene, medical technology, living conditions, and life expectancy all contributed to this enormous growth.

Many have raised concerns about the capacity of one planet to support human life at these levels. Gretchen C. Daily and Paul R. Ehrlich published a helpful article in the November 1992 issue of *Bioscience*, pointing out that the sustainable carrying capacity was highest when only biophysical issues were analyzed and was lower when social differences were considered. Social differences involve personal life decisions for every inhabitant and different socioeconomic concerns for a nation. It's an overwhelming task to figure out a good outcome while trading off incentives that may sacrifice the future for the present.

Experts believe that population will continue to grow at a diminishing rate to about 12 billion by the year 2150. Estimates of world population are as follows:

YEAR	2000	2010	2020	2030	2040	2050	2100	2150
Billions	6.08	6.87	7.66	8.37	9.00	9.55	11.31	12.02

Over the last thirty years, there has been significant controversy on the subject of world population and its challenges. What are the concerns, and what can we do about it? The challenge is to provide adequate supplies of land, top soil, ground water, nutrients, minerals, metals, energy, and food. The analysis is complicated and is often solved anecdotally or with simplified assumptions. The debate ranges from "technology will solve all the concerns" to "we are already over-populated because we are consuming all the nonrenewable energy."

Solving population growth is challenging because the world is splintered into nations with governments that use the Conquer and Oppress doctrine. Instead of following an affordable strategy with action plans over time that produce a good ROI, wedge issues dominate our national discussion.

A good example is global warming. It has been singled out as a looming crisis by Al Gore and funded by a few parties with vested interests. These special interests contribute to political campaigns. The politicians then fund pet programs and start telling corporations like General Motors how to run their businesses. The end result is market share loss that leads to bankruptcy. Until we develop a national strategic plan based on free market capitalism that makes sense, we will not be able to balance good programs against bad. Furthermore we can't empower other nations to do the right thing when our own policies and programs are prioritized from minority interests instead of strategic priorities that emphasize GDP growth.

Our world today is home to about 6.8 billion people. This is a fifteen-fold increase from 438 million in the year 1500. In addition we have achieved increasing improvements in wealth, health, technology, and productivity. Unfortunately there have been enough corrupt and incompetent governments using failed policies, that today many inequities exist in living standards throughout the world.

In most countries the population growth rate is a function of the birth rate, death rate, and life expectancy. Immigration plays a minor role. The outstanding exception is America. Population growth for the United States exceeds that of all other nations by a significant amount. For 150 years immigration and assimilation has played an important role in the dynamism and economic success of America. I call this free market immigration.

Historical World Population

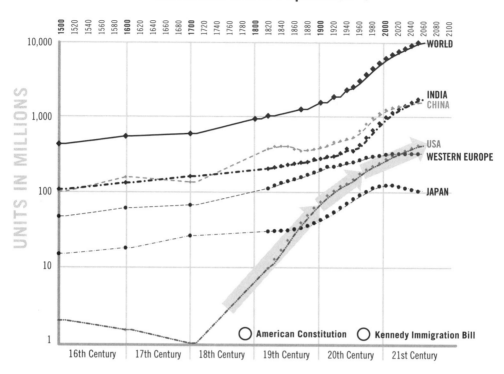

Population growth for America, shown in the chart above, slows significantly in the twentieth century. Clearly public policy combined with the change in immigration law in 1965 favoring family over education and job skills has created slower growth and chaotic immigration.

It will become clear as we explore the major elements of a strategic plan that GDP growth will be our highest priority. Our minimum growth must be at the world GDP rate in order to maintain our leading market share. America's immigration policy should support a commitment to achieve the growth rate set by the strategic plan. Even with reasonable productivity growth we will need to significantly increase our population with a variety of job skills to meet the GDP objective. Government policy should establish an annual goal for the issuance of green cards that fits the strategic plan. Businesses must be given the freedom to hire the skills they need, when they need them, and from wherever they choose to recruit them. Green cards provide immigrants with permanent resident status with most of the privileges of citizenship. Citizenship can be applied for after five years.

Prior to 1965 immigration levels were established by country of origin, businesses were free to hire skilled people from those countries, and the priority was based on education level and job skills. Unfortunately this was changed dramatically in 1965 with a bill sponsored by Ted Kennedy. In this bill levels of immigration were set on a worldwide basis without consideration for country of origin and the highest priority was based on family relationship.

For most of the twentieth century, the unions put pressure on politicians to limit the number of green card immigrants in direct conflict with the needs of business. Our politicians who are now masters of the Machiavellian compromise tinkered with compromise visas like H1 and guest worker programs to appease the unions. An H1 visa requires the worker to immigrate for one specific job and then return to the country of origin when the job is over. These programs do not work. If a skillful person decides to accept a compromise visa, he is most likely going to stay permanently even if it means a period of illegal status. Another policy that has unintended consequences is that citizenship is granted to babies born in the United States even if the parents have illegal status.

The unintended consequences of these liberal policies, written into law by career politicians, corrupted by special interests, have been catastrophic for our country and our economy. Our politicians put special interests ahead of economic results. The end result was to create chaos and redistribute wealth. Over time millions of illegal immigrants poured over our borders to fill only some of the jobs needed for a high growth GDP. Important jobs went unfilled, and granting benefits to illegal aliens placed an extreme burden on our education and healthcare systems. This policy has made our nation poorer during the last sixty years. I leave it to you to decide whether this was unintended or whether certain politicians saw it as a way to change the political landscape.

In the twenty-first century, nation states are governed in many ways from dictatorships to democracies. In most cases, current government is a remnant of traditional methods left over from centuries of experiments by powerful leaders. These methods may have worked for extended periods but were not ultimately sustainable. All the methods tried to date have failed or are failing. America's democracy, created by the Founding Fathers, coupled with free market capitalism, and supported by aggressive job-related immigration policies, has demonstrated the most promise for future prosperity and peace for our world.

Historically, growth has been achieved by powerful people taking control of a community, setting up rules, regulations, religions, controls, and methods for reward or punishment. Often, without checks and balances, this approach resulted in an elite leadership and an impoverished-enslaved underclass. Many nations that were productive using totalitarian government often built a military to expand territorially. Expansion occurred by attacking other nations, plundering their riches, killing those who would threaten the new expanded nation, and enslaving the remaining men, women, and children. In order to minimize revolution from below, the leadership provided law and order with carrots to control the few, and sticks to control the many. Sticks were often applied by using brutal punishment to control the population.

Today it is clear that people are our most important and valuable asset. All the people of the world must be treated with respect and encouraged to learn, grow, and change for the benefit of mankind. The future can be bright if we support *Compete and Empower* as the way to proceed.

IMPROVE PROSPERITY FOR ALL THE PEOPLE

In presenting a better approach to prosperity and peace, one that includes a growing workforce that can change skills with the needs of the world marketplace, we must consider limitations to world population. Forecasts of GDP growth and productivity in this chapter will take into account our world's carrying capacity to support human life. It is a complex subject and more anecdotal than analytic. Carrying capacity includes both biophysical and social carrying capacities and be sustainable now and for future generations.

Why is this topic confusing? Because on the one hand we have the United Nations (UN) suggesting that world population could reach 12 billion by 2150. On the other we have authors Jones and Wigley, and Schneider, suggesting that we are already exceeding the world's current social carrying capacity and are depleting resources necessary to meet future needs. Because of the ingenuity and spirit of peoples around the world, I will assume that we will find a way to support 12 billion humans by 2150.

America's, and the world's, first priority is to improve the growth of world GDP so that enough wealth is generated to raise the average productivity per person in the world above the poverty line. In 2008 the world GDP grew to $52 trillion, the population was about 6.8 billion and the average productivity (wealth) per person was $7,600 per year. In the United States we consider $10,000 per year the poverty line, as I've mentioned previously. 81 percent or 5.5 billion of the world's population lives below the poverty line. This is disgraceful and is an indictment of the Conquer and Oppress policies of world governments. My strategic plan in Chapter 8 will free up the people to become more self-reliant, free up the market to develop powerful products with curb appeal, free up government control so that the people and their businesses are in charge, and raise everyone's standard of living.

There is only one way to improve the life of people around the world. We, the people, must increase the GDP faster than the growth of population. Rapid growth comes from growing profits so that the people have excess capital to reinvest. I have imagined three future scenarios and assumptions in order to see if there are outcomes that will improve the wealth and prosperity of all the people. The following table shows the increase in wealth per person by 2050 for three different values of world GDP growth.

Three Scenarios of World GDP Growth

World Scenario	2010 GDP	2050 GDP	Annual Growth	2010 People	2050 People	2010 GDP $ per Person	2050 GDP $ per Person
#1	$51.0B	$202B	3.5%	6.87B	9.55B	$7,427	$21,155
#2	$50.8B	$358B	5.0%	6.87B	9.55B	$7,398	$37,477
#3	$50.8B	$523B	6.0%	6.87B	9.55B	$7,398	$54,760

I'm basing the first scenario on current expert opinion data, which is usually based on historical facts and trends. Incremental estimates are then made based on existing trends, with little deviation assuming present government policies continue. The Bureau of Economic Analysis (BEA) and the United States Department of Agriculture (USDA) tracks a lot of economic data and reports changes regularly. They also make forecasts of economic trends based on this data. This approach is risk adverse based on current trends and statistics. Because of the current crisis, forecasters are quite pessimistic. Therefore this is a low risk poor return plan because the growth is not high enough to support acceptable increases in wealth for the average person.

My second scenario is based on strategic intent, which is a main focus of this book. I assume the world will continue to grow at 5 percent. This is consistent with world GDP growth over the last fifty years. Using reasonable growth in productivity, (3 percent), GDP per person reaches $37,477. This is a good return realistic risk plan.

The third scenario requires "thinking outside the box." The assumptions used are considered outliers and suggest ambitious growth, resulting in an aggressive strategic plan. The focus is on rapid increase of GDP. This is an exceptional return high risk plan where wealth per person reaches $54,760 by 2050. Although I believe world GDP can grow at higher rates than historical performance, by unleashing the potential of the people around the world with a *Compete and Empower* philosophy, scenario three is unlikely to garner much support because of the pessimism of our experts.

Before we progress to the next section about people, I must introduce an important tool called the experience curve.

EXPERIENCE CURVE

In the early part of the twentieth century, many manufacturing companies found that when their volume of production increased, their cost of production came down. This became known as the manufacturing learning curve. For every doubling of production, the cost to manufacture fell a fixed percentage. Typical learning curves were 5 percent to 15 percent depending on the type of manufacturing.

W. Edwards Deming introduced Total Quality Management (TQM) to the Japanese in the early 1980s. His fourteen point philosophy was that if the whole company was involved in fixing quality problems and introducing the fixes into operations, then costs would come down and quality would go up. A commitment to this TQM process became a competitive strategy for many companies. Before Deming introduced these ideas in the 1950s the standard was to not to fix the problem but to test for failures and scrap the stuff that did not past muster.

Bruce Henderson observed in his analysis of natural competition that the experience curve, related to TQM, could make a company very competitive. The organization that understood this and got the entire organization behind the strategic plan would reduce all operating costs and improve the quality of the customer experience, and increase the company's competiveness. The experience curve applies to all operations of the company so that all costs go down a fixed percent for each doubling of volume. 25 percent to 40 percent experience curves are not unheard of.

It is easy to see why since the 1960s the union movement has been destructive to any company it is involved with. The CEO's goal is to encourage all employees to support the strategic plan and to be actively involved in providing the best customer experience possible. Because of this teamwork, the company will be highly competitive by using the experience curve to reduce costs and improve quality for customer benefit. The union's goal is to enroll some of the employees, who perform a few of the jobs required, in the union. Then the union bosses set up the employees to be in conflict with management. Management is pressured to pay more in compensation and benefits than market rates suggest for the jobs they represent, and in addition they demand restrictive work rules. If management will not play ball, they threaten strikes or work stoppages. None of these actions are helpful to the company's competitive strategy. Teamwork is destroyed.

Because this chapter is about people, and the people of America will have a significant effect on world wealth and prosperity, it is appropriate to take a look at the current situation to help us prepare for the courageous changes we must make to ensure America leads the twenty-first century.

CAN AMERICA RECOVER FROM THE CURRENT CRISIS AND RESUME THE OUTSTANDING PERFORMANCE OF ITS PEOPLE AND THEIR BUSINESSES?

America is at a cross road and must be careful about its choice of road ahead. As an immigrant to this country in 1960, I am both an observer of and a believer in the American principles that made us great. We stand today as the best-performing democracy the world has ever known. Yet we have a cancer in our midst. Our politicians and our government are not working for the best of America and its people. They have violated the oaths they've taken to honor and support the constitution. There are conflicts of interest between their career goals and what's best for the people.

I would like to take this time to analyze the current situation, determine if it is a threat to the republic, and end on an optimistic note that the future looks bright if we have the courage to act now.

THE CURRENT SITUATION

Politicians are panicking over the current financial crisis and behaving badly. Many articles have been written about the inability of politicians and their government staff to comprehend basic business practices. In order to show how out of control our government and politicians have become, I analyzed information from BEA, USDA, Wikipedia, and www. usgovernmentspending.com. The data analysis I made focused on four year increments that coincide with the last year of a presidents four year term, as well as the size and growth rate of GDP for the World.

First we should acknowledge the outstanding performance of our business people.

There are approximately 300 million people, 125 million employees, and 25 million businesses in the United States. 100 million people of the 125 million employed are investors.

Some are small investors who participate through their 401Ks and pension funds; others are large investors who represent the wealthiest people in the nation.

Individuals, small businesses, and large corporations are the only source of wealth and prosperity for America. Government, on the other hand, is a drag on our prosperity. The 100 million employee investors are the only source of funds to invest in stocks, bonds, and real estate and at the same time they pay the taxes to fund the government. While business investments are highly regulated and their performance measured, government projects, paid for by the taxes we pay, are poorly documented, rarely measured, and have no ROI. Our government should play by the same rules it requires business to follow.

At the end of Nixon's first term in 1972, America's GDP stood at $4.2 trillion. By the end of Bush's second term America's GDP was $13.2 trillion, a more than 300 percent growth! While there were periods of underperformance and periods of over performance along the way, the bottom line is that American business people found ways to grow their businesses in spite of meddling by politicians. America's market share of world GDP held at 26.7 percent in 2007, down only slightly from 27.2 percent in 1972. We had grown at a rate similar to the growth rate of world GDP.

China's performance was also superb. Its GDP grew from $0.1 to $3.1 trillion over the same time period. Because of its strategic intent to make GDP growth the country's highest priority, China grew at 9.5 percent, twice the world GDP growth rate of 5.0 percent. Market share grew from 0.1 percent to 6.3 percent by 2007. Because of this performance, and because the Washington crowd doesn't have a clue how business works, U.S. politicians have declared defeat and now herald the twenty-first century as the Chinese Century. They run around in panic, hold show trials in Congress, blame business people for crises the government created, and denigrate the very people who make it possible to pay taxes and create wealth and prosperity for all the people.

Over the last fifty years, there have been literally thousands and thousands of strategic plan success stories. Companies like Apple, HP, IBM, Intel, TI, Wal-Mart, GE, Johnson Controls, P&G, Amgen, and Berkshire Hathaway are just a few. These companies are resilient and high performing. All employees work together as a team in a symbiotic relationship between customers and investors. Customers write the checks for beneficial products, investors provide the capital for company growth in exchange for a good return, and employees innovate by reducing cost and improving quality as they go down the experience curve. Growth provides more jobs with increasing compensation for all employees as responsibility grows.

The failures like GM stand out because they did not follow good business practice. Eighty years ago the company was given an outstanding start by its founders and the company grew quickly, claiming over 60 percent of the domestic market share. For the last fifty years, GM has been losing market share until 2009, when it filed for bankruptcy.

How did this happen?

A number of factors brought GM to its knees. Complacency set in within the higher echelons of management. They succumbed to union demands that increased their cost and reduced their quality for a few specific job descriptions. This prevented GM from moving down the experience curve. Management was then squeezed by politicians who dictated what type of cars GM should make. Michigan became a union state, which did not help because right-to-work states like Tennessee have a significant advantage. Management should have been courageous enough to tell the unions and politicians that unless this nonsense stops they would bankrupt the Michigan operations and start again in locations more favorable to business success.

Let us go back to the high-performance companies. They became high-performance companies by realizing that each job description, out of thousands in a large company, may need specific compensation to maximize results. CEOs charged their human resource departments and compensation committees to come up with imaginative ways to provide motivation and incentives. Because there are so many types of jobs there are many types of compensation. An hourly worker may be paid by the hour or paid on how much work was completed. In addition, a profit-sharing bonus may be paid to encourage the hourly employee to be a team player. A sales person may get a low base pay and a high commission. A technical employee may be offered a lower base pay with a bonus based on meeting certain project objectives. A CEO may get stock options that vest over years to encourage corporate initiatives that benefit the shareholders.

Incentive compensation provides a significant competitive advantage and should be considered carefully by anyone privy to company confidential information. The bottom line credibility in all these methods of compensation is to base compensation on market studies of the free market value of a specific job. Corporations set their policies based on this target compensation and adjust incentive programs by reducing base and adding incentives. Such programs are considered intellectual property that keeps the company competitive.

Knowing this, it is beyond imagination how an incompetent politician can propose a law that will tax certain bonuses at 90 percent in certain types of companies. It is so ignorant of the facts. That politician is acting on the premise that if he pontificates enough he may get some extra votes at election time. He ignores the unintended consequence: putting the company out of business, thereby reducing the taxes available to pay his salary.

Now let us take a look at the spending performance of our politicians.

Federal government spending from 1972 to 2008 has been completely out of control. At the turn of the last century, before Roosevelt corrupted the system with excessive taxes, federal spending was less than 1 percent. Back in 1972 when Nixon finished his first term, federal government spending was $0.231 trillion, 5 percent of a $4.2 trillion GDP. By the end of Carter's term in 1980, government spending had risen to 10.1 percent of GDP. In my view total federal government spending should not go over 11 percent, 5 percent for protection, 5 percent for overhead, and 1 percent for safety net purposes. Most self-respecting conglomerates run with 5 percent corporate overhead. Berkshire Hathaway runs with a lot less!

By 2008 at the end of Bush's term government spending was $3.0 trillion, a whopping 22.6 percent of GDP. This amount does include spending on Social Security and Medicare. The citizens were told by politicians that Social Security and Medicare were to be funded by withholding money from their income along with an equal contribution to be made by the company the people worked for. Instead of putting this money into an investment fund where it would stand alone as a balance sheet item, politicians preferred to put the money into the general funds so they could spend it on pet projects of social engineering. To make matters worse they covered up their obfuscation by telling their citizens that the payments would be called mandatory spending programs. What they withheld was that they could change the benefits if the spending got too high.

What do we get for federal spending?

We get a bloated unionized government payroll, schools that produce poorer and poorer performance for more and more money, a post office that cannot compete with FedEx and UPS, a Ponzi Social Security system managed by politicians who renege on commitments to stay solvent, and Medicare that is out of control.

There is one redeeming feature to our government, and that's the fact that our military is the finest force of fighting personnel, backed up with the greatest technology the world has ever known. Unfortunately politicians enjoy taking resources from what works and giving the resources to those activities that don't. The politicians cut back on military investments in our safety and write checks for programs that are not working, and then have the gall to sell it as a peace dividend in a very unsafe world.

Perhaps there is a silver lining in the "end of presidential term data" that I analyzed. The Clinton presidential years, combined with a Republican Congress led by Gingrich, showed that America could grow faster than world GDP and constrain spending at the same time. These results may provide a guide to circumvent the inevitable dark clouds ahead created by out-of-control government spending. It is interesting to note that during Clinton's two terms, ending in 1996 and 2000, when he was pragmatic enough to compromise with a very conservative Republican House and Senate, together they achieved the only period where spending fell slightly as a percent of GDP. At the end of Bush I term, spending was 16.7 percent of GDP. At the end of Clinton's first term when the Republican Contract with America swept Gingrich in as speaker with control of Congress, spending fell to 16.6 percent of GDP. At the end of Clinton's second term-spending was 16.1 percent of GDP. Also in that period we grew faster than world GDP rate of growth.

We, the people, should be very concerned about the current situation. What should have proceeded as an orderly profes-sional process in the second half of 2008 to slowly reduce debt and leverage in the financial community became a tipping point. When Lehman Brothers collapsed, secretary of the Treasury under the Bush administration panicked and made an emergency request to Congress for $700 billion. This was immediately approved by a stampeding Democrat-controlled Congress to fix a banking fiasco caused by the politicians. This in turn created a global downward spiral of critical proportions. Now we have a new administration that's throwing large amounts of money we do not have at the problem, hoping to stabilize the market. Because of our economic dominance in world markets, our panic triggered a tipping point for the rest of the world. Because the majority of the rest of the world has socialist type governments they did not have the tools or flexibility to stop the crisis affecting their economies. If it continues America's federal spending at 28 percent to 35 percent of GDP will crush the American dream. So what's to be done?

On the one hand, we have political leaders who are devastating the current financial situation, diminishing America's future, and precipitating one more civilization's demise. On the other hand, the performance of our people and their businesses has been superb over the last century. With the Constitution as our guiding light, we have performed against all odds. All we need to do is remove most of the current political leaders from office and replace them with civic-minded citizens who would be honored to serve the people as public servants for only one eight-year term. This change will fix the current malaise, but it will take a lot of courage to save America. Read on for some positive ideas we can use to make a difference. Prosperity is our next subject. Working hard to accumulate wealth is important to building a successful life for ourselves and our family, but not as important as leading a prosperous life where we achieve other goals that fit our passions.

CHAPTER THREE

PROSPERITY

Wealth to survive and freedom to choose one's own journey

Prosperity through peace is a worthy goal. Some will say it's impossible, but it's not. Powerful countries can compete with honor without the need to conquer and kill. Success stories told from the Olympics are good examples of peaceful competition. Prosperity is about choices. The choices we make about wealth and goals will determine whether we lead a life of passion and purpose, or whether we just drift from day to day.

From an economic perspective, prosperity starts with wealth. Does a person earn enough to cover the basic needs, and is there some left over to invest in additional goals? Saving to purchase income-generating assets, going back to school to learn more skills, and pursuing subjects of passion are all ways to lead a prosperous life.

The wealth of a nation and its people comes from the peoples businesses. The GDP of a nation is the value received from all the products and services delivered by the people and the businesses. Wealth is determined by dividing GDP by the country's population. In 2005 America ranked 8th out of 192 nations at $42,000 per person. Less than $10,000 per person means that person is living in poverty.

According to http://earthtrends.wri.org, a Web site that tracks approximately two hundred nations, the GDP per person for the year 2005 ranges from $100 to $78,000. The following table shows the distribution of prosperity:

Top Ten	$39,000 to $78,000
11th to 50th	$11,000 to $39,000
51st to 100th	$ 2,750 to $11,000
101st to 200th	$100 to $2,750

Top Ten Nations in Productivity

Rank	Nation	Populaton	Productvity
1	Luxembourg	464,904	$78,428
2	Norway	4,751,236	$63,964
3	Iceland	309,672	$53,607
4	Qatar	812,842	$52,230
5	Switzerland	7,252,331	$50,611
6	Ireland	4,147,901	$48,654
7	Denmark	5,471,590	$47,637
8	America	301,140,000	$41,636
9	Sweden	9,041,262	$39,562
10	Bermuda (UK)	64,174	$39,600

2005 Data

This uneven distribution is based on the productivity of the people and the performance of their nation's governments. Twenty-five years ago Ireland would have been ranked significantly lower as a backward rural country, but through superior strategy that focused on high GDP growth and lower taxes, it's reached the ranking of #6 in the world, higher than the United States. If only our politicians were smart enough to do the right thing for our people.

It should be noted that in the financial crisis of 2008/2009 Ireland and Iceland have suffered substantially, because they borrowed too much to support the high growth rates and invested in too many risky derivative securities. Only time will tell if they are nimble and careful enough to stabilize the country's finances and continue a path to prosperity for their people.

American politicians have squandered the wealth of the people over the last eighty years by taking control of the country, confiscating exorbitant taxes and wasting the money on social engineering programs to get re-elected. The war on poverty continues with no end in sight, other than more spending. This lack of accountability is a major reason for America's ranking of eight, out of the top ten in wealth/GDP per person. The high growth rate and market share achieved by our citizens and their businesses is worthy of the number one ranking position above $80,000 per person.

I can remember arriving in the United States in 1960 as an entry-level engineer. My starting salary was $7,200—three times my British salary. More importantly, I could buy a top-of-the-line, Buick Electra for $2,500, one third of my salary. Today an entry-level engineer would make $30,000 in salary, and would pay more than $30,000 for a top-of-the-line Buick Sedan.

According to a dictionary, prosperity is "the state of being prosperous." Prosperity encompasses an advance or gain in anything good or desirable personally, commercially, or nationally. Other helpful descriptions are personal success, good fortune, reaching objectives, or implementing a successful business.

A useful way to determine an individual's prosperity is to consider Maslow's hierarchy of needs and recognize that individuals will come to their own conclusions on what works for their aspirations. One person may be completely content at level 1 with life's basic needs taken care of, whereas another won't be content until he reaches level 5. Throughout one's life, a person's aspirations may change. The level chosen during the child support years may well be different when the children leave the nest.

MASLOW'S HIERARCHY OF NEEDS

(5) Self-actualization personal needs growth and fulfillment

(4) Esteem needs Achievement, status, responsibility, reputation

(3) Belongingness and love needs Family, affection, relationships, workgroup, etc.

(2) Safety needs Protection, security, order, law, limits, stability, etc.

(1) Biological and physiological needs (Basic life needs)—air, food, drink, shelter, etc.

PERSONAL PROSPERITY

What is the path to prosperity for an individual? First come the childhood years, when your family and society invest in your future.

If you are lucky your family has the resources to invest heavily in your early growth and education and your society is a free and successful democracy. If you are unlucky, your family is dysfunctional and has limited resources for child rearing and education, and your society limits the prosperity of its citizens.

In either case, if you understand that the human experience is almost infinite, and realize this is only the beginning of a long and purposeful life, you will make the circumstances work for you. Becoming an adult is getting through Maslow's level 1 and surviving by being self-sufficient. In one case you may be in your twenties with advanced degrees, in the other in your teens with barely a high school education. Both are just early milestones in a lifelong journey. There is no right or wrong, better, or worse, path to prosperity.

You may find yourself in a restrictive society that limits your opportunity to move through Maslow's level 2. In that case it's helpful to remember that change is the only constant in a successful life. In order to move beyond level 2, you may need to change jobs, areas, regions, or nations to find your path to prosperity. Because the world around us continues to change, accept change as an enjoyable attribute of a purposeful life.

You can move through Maslow's levels 3, 4, and 5 by being productive, growing every day, and being financially smart by reading and applying ideas presented by Robert Kiyosaki in his book *Rich Dad, Poor Dad*. He said, "Do not be an employee all your life while increasing your lifestyle (spending) at every turn. Set a low lifestyle spending pattern when you are young. Earn more than your living expenses and invest the difference in income generating assets. When the income from your investment assets exceeds your living expenses you become free." You can pursue your passions and dreams by following Robert's simple philosophy "Pay yourself first."

There are many examples of this type of success. In Los Gatos, California, in the 1980s, a seventeen-year-old convinced a few family members and friends to loan him the down payment on a house across the street from the high school. He moved into the house and persuaded a number of other students to move in, pay rent, and contribute to the improvement and maintenance of the property. By his late twenties he owned a number of properties. He had become a millionaire.

After childhood come the adult years, a time when one can produce more than one's needs and therefore contribute to both oneself and to society. Over a lifetime individuals can move up through Maslow's hierarchy of needs until they've achieved their definition of personal prosperity. Also, because change is constant, some people may fall back down Maslow's hierarchy of needs. Self-sufficient, empowered individuals will understand the risks they have taken and will rise again to achieve personal prosperity.

SOCIETAL OR NATIONAL PROSPERITY

National prosperity is based on the character and prosperity of its people the freedom, and transparency of its method of government, and the quality of its leaders.

Throughout history, most societies and nations tended to start with a leader who took control by exercising power. The leader then appointed a ruling class, obedient to the leader's direction. This elite class often controlled the general population with oppressive rules and regulations, excessive taxation, torture, and enslavement. Although religions provide a framework of morals for a just society, religion often became oppressive to retain its power. If the ruling class lost control of its citizens, then revolution occurred. The people terminated the elite class, took over control, and the cycle began again.

In order to prosper, a nation must generate increasing wealth and freedom for the citizens. Popular experiments for expansion include imperialism, colonialism, communism, socialism, and free market capitalism. Although some of these concepts may have "appeared" to work for hundreds of years, history has shown that all of them, except free market capitalism, have failed or are in the process of failing.

For everyone to prosper, society must support the philosophy that from growth comes wealth and from wealth comes prosperity. In today's nations we measure wealth by the size of the nation's GDP and the nation's growth rate. The growth of wealth is more than a first priority. It is like breathing. Without breathing we wither and die. Without growth a nation will do the same.

In a free society protected from outside aggression, where the citizen has the opportunity to continuously increase his personal wealth, each person is free to choose any level on Maslow's hierarchy and feel prosperous at that level.

THE EFFECT OF GROSS DOMESTIC PRODUCT

GDP is a useful measure of wealth because it is measured frequently, widely, and consistently and can be used to understand productivity and world market share. Sometimes it is criticized for not covering all the nuances of a particular subject, but it creates a good comparative base for evaluating strategy. We have shown that personal prosperity is achieved by choosing a level of wealth for freedom and a level of satisfaction from Maslow's hierarchy. We will now develop an understanding of GDP and its components so that we can unravel the relationship between material, labor, profit, capital, and yield.

In a peaceful world where businesses emphasize the *Compete and Empower* philosophy, there is a symbiotic relationship between customers, employees, and investors. All participants of a strategy-driven endeavor must get a good experience and a fair return from the investments. All the employees working together in support of the strategic plan will increase market share, quality, and the customer experience while reducing cost. Customers benefit from the value of the products they purchase. Growing the company and profits supports its shareholders with excellent returns, thereby reducing the cost of capital. This symbiotic relationship between all constituents is the most efficient path to peaceful wealth and prosperity.

Unfortunately, in those nations that continue to use Conquer and Oppress, there is a divisive, and sometimes dysfunctional, relationship between labor and capital. Leaders who perpetuate divisive ideas are stuck in the past, mainly interested in retaining their power. They are not open to a better, more peaceful future by encouraging our people to grow, grow, grow, change, change, change, and commit to cooperation between employee labor and capital. Instead, our leaders preach to the population about two Americas, the rich versus the poor, the elites versus the workers. Conducting class warfare is intellectually dishonest, reduces competitive performance, and enslaves many workers in welfare.

In the early days, individuals started as hunters or gatherers, but once they were productive enough to provide for their families, they began producing more than they needed. They specialized and traded or bartered within the tribe. As time went on tribes specialized, and then collected together, in a region or nation so they could trade with each other. Eventually they formed nations to protect their population from other nations and to increase their wealth through trade.

Today we have workers who develop special skills and band together into corporations to provide products focused on high value consumer needs. The value of the work, skill, and product fluctuate as a function of the supply and demand. Over time the skills and products with the highest values change and require substantial changes in worker and corporate skills, location, and product benefits. Hence the need for all parties to embrace change and not fight it, as union management has done in the past.

The first method for calculating GDP, and perhaps the most popular, is the consumption method. In this case GDP is the sum of private consumption (the consumer), government spending (employee salary, expense, and equipment), investment spending (equipment, facilities, and construction to improve productivity), and exports with imports deducted. See the following table for an example of the United States's GDP.

GDP for the United States by Consumption

	2007	2006	2005
Private Consumption	$9,710.200	$9,207.225	$8,694.125
Business Investments in Capital	$2,130.300	$2,220.350	$2,086.100
Government Expenditures	$2,674.800	$2,508.100	$2,355.275
Taxes	$1,662.400	$1,480.750	$1,311.500
<Subsidies>	($2,370.200)	($2,238.075)	($2,025.125)
Total GDP	$13,807.500	$13,178.350	$12,421.875

Data by www.econstats.com. $ in billions.

The second method for calculating GDP is the income method most often referred to as Gross National Product (GNP). In this case GNP is the sum of income earned by employees (labor), gross operating surplus (corporate profit), gross mixed income (small business profit), and taxes with subsidies on production and imports deducted. See the table below for an example of the United States's GNP.

GNP for the United States by Income

	2007	2006	2005
Employee Compensation & Other Expense	$12,270.900	$11,795.725	$10,974.000
Corporation Profit	$1,192.000	$1,199.625	$1,034.250
Corporation Taxes	$450.400	$468.900	$413.700
Small Business Profit	$1,056.200	$1,014.700	$959.825
Other Taxes, Items <Subsidies>	($1,162.000)	($1,300.600)	($959.900)
Total GNP	$13,807.500	$13,178.350	$12,421.875

Data by www.econstats.com. $ in billions.

Now that we have GDP defined by consumption and income, let's explore the components of labor and capital in their relationship to a typical business.

A successful company is in business to prosper. For this to happen, the company's strategic plan must provide growth, wealth, and prosperity for all its constituents—the customers, shareholders, and employees. Customers benefit from outstanding competitive products or services that fit their changing needs. Shareholders who provide the capital benefit by getting a good return/yield with reasonable risk on their investment. Employees benefit by getting competitive wages and benefits for high-quality work in the many job skills required to operate the company. In most companies there are many job skills required at rising levels of compensation. An additional benefit is available to the employee who is committed to grow and change. That person can significantly increase his wealth by growing from job to job. I am sure you have heard the story many times of the mail boy who seized the opportunity to grow and change and ended up the company president.

The corporate role is to acquire (buy), operate (use), and liquidate (sell) assets for the benefit of shareholders. The business role is to develop (purchase), value engineer (evolve), and manufacture (produce) products, or services for the benefit of customers.

To ensure prosperity, many companies develop their five to ten year strategic plans around mid-fiscal year and put together operating plans for the next year in the fourth quarter. One job of the CEO is to communicate the strategic and operating plans to all levels of the company and encourage the employees to fully support them. This encourages teamwork so the left hand knows what the right hand is doing. It also improves the likelihood that all the constituents will prosper.

The strategic plan will focus a company's resources on the best product fit for a specific market segment where the company can dominate. In addition it will point out the most important assets and job skills that warrant emphasis to compete effectively. The company may choose to outsource basic skills or functions as a more productive use of company resources. A good strategic plan will focus all key resources on the vision and strategy while prioritizing them to ensure overall success.

The operating plan enables the organization to deliver on its commitment to produce a great customer experience, an empowering work environment and a good return on capital by meeting the financial goals. The annual operating plan establishes commitment to specific objectives and financial results month by month and quarter by quarter. Meeting or exceeding this plan enables the company to reach new levels of prosperity.

Let us now look at a typical company Profit/<Loss> Pro-Forma (P/<L>) to discuss the symbiotic relationship between capital and employee labor and how wedge issues raised by politicians and union bosses may be counterproductive.

Profit/<Loss> Pro-Forma for a Typical Business Summary

	YEAR 1	%	YEAR 2	%
Sales (Revenue)	$10.000		$20.000	100.0%
			Experience Curve	10.0%
Total Cost of Goods Sold (COGS)	$5.000	50.0%	$9.000	45.0%
Research & Development (R&D)	$1.000	10.0%	$1.800	9.0%
Marketing	$0.400	4.0%	$0.720	3.6%
Sales	$1.600	16.0%	$2.880	14.4%
General & Administration (G&A)	$1.000	10.0%	$1.800	9.0%
Total Operating Expense	$4.000	40.0%	$7.200	36.0%
Profit /<Loss> Before Tax (BT)	**$1.000**	**10.0%**	**$3.800**	**19.0%**
Corporate Tax	$0.350	35.0%	$1.330	35.0%
Profit /<Loss> After Tax (AT)	**$0.650**	**6.5%**	**$2.470**	**12.4%**

$ in millions.

The P/<L> shows the relationship of spending (investment) in developing and marketing the product, selling, and producing the product, managing the enterprise, and returning a profit to pay for the capital used. By showing two years with a doubling of sales, a growth of 100 percent, we can consider the effect of the experience curve and productivity of operations. The balance sheet information shown below provides information on capital requirements so that we can discuss why employee labor and capital should be a cooperative relationship.

Balance Sheet Pro-Forma for a Typical Business Detail

	YEAR 1	%	YEAR 2	%
		Experience Curve		10.0%
Total Assets	**$4.000**	**40.0%**	**$7.200**	**36.0%**
Cash	$0.200	2.0%	$0.360	1.8%
Receivables	$1.700	17.0%	$3.060	15.3%
Inventory	$1.100	11.0%	$1.980	9.9%
Net Capital Equipment	$1.000	10.0%	$1.800	9.0%
Total Liabilities	**$0.500**	**5.0%**	**$0.900**	**4.5%**
Short-Term Financing	$0.100	1.0%	$0.180	0.9%
Payables	$0.200	2.0%	$0.360	1.8%
Long-Term Debt	$0.200	2.0%	$0.360	1.8%
Net Worth	**$3.500**		**$6.300**	
Paid in Capital	$6.000		$6.330	
Start Up Loss	($3.150)		($3.150)	
Retained Earnings Current Year	$0.650		$2.470	
Retained Earnings Accumulated	($2.500)		($0.030)	
		Capital		**Capital**
Profit /<Loss> AT	**$0.650**	**10.8%**	**$2.470**	**39.0%**

$ in millions.

In this example it took $6.0 million in capital to reach $10.0 million in sales including start-up costs and Year 3 profit after tax. Therefore the yield on capital is 10.8 percent in Year 3. It took the first two years to develop the product and introduce it to the market.

Now let us look under the hood. The P/<L> above show five categories of cost (expenses). They are cost of goods sold, research, and development, marketing, sales, and general and administrative. If we were to see a detailed report of each element for each category, we would find that there are employees in every category, with hundreds of job descriptions. This detailed report would show that all the employee labor adds up to 58 percent of sales or $5.8 million for Year 3. The total labor clearly covers a wide range of job skills. One of the CEO's tasks is to make sure that the plans of the company are well understood and every employee pulls together as a team. In Year 3, at $10 million in revenue the competitive value of these jobs could range from an entry level position at $15,000 per year to the CEO at $160,000 per year, a 10 to 1 range.

In this example the Year 4 performance improved on Year 3's. Sales doubled to $20 million, all functions of the company reduced costs on a 10 percent experience curve, and the after tax profit increased to $2.47 million (12.4 percent) up from one year earlier at $0.65 million (6.5 percent). Note that the full spectrum of employee labor expense increased to $10.53 million (52.7 percent) from $5.85 million (58.5 percent). This performance increased jobs, job skills, and job accountability. The entry level job was still valued at $15,000 but the CEO position may be now worth $750,000 based on pay for performance and a combination of profit bonuses and stock option appreciation. This is now a 50-to-1 range from top to bottom. As the company grows, it requires more jobs with higher skills, those higher job descriptions require higher levels of accountability and higher levels of compensation.

Unscrupulous media individuals and partisan politicians may use this 50-to-1 statistic to mislead the unsuspecting worker, claiming that this gap is unfair. Clearly the entry level job compensation did not change much from year to year, yet neither did the job itself. Perhaps it changed by a small amount due to inflation. The CEO job, along with other jobs that required more responsibility, deserved to be paid at market rates based on the increase in sales. The unscrupulous claim the rich are getting richer on the backs of the worker. Union management claim that the entry-level job should be paid more money and benefits than the job is worth.

An entry-level employee who embraces a philosophy of personal growth and acceptance to change will not accept these false premises and join the union, but will learn new skills so he can move to a new job paying a higher salary.

If the employee had followed the "pay yourself first philosophy" mentioned earlier and set his living expenses so that he could invest 10 percent of his income into income, generating assets, then the employee is committed to grow toward freedom. The employee benefits from more opportunity to grow and becomes more prosperous as the company grows.

What has been described so far is an environment where self-reliant, growth-oriented individuals, who understand that change is part of life, band together into successful businesses (corporations) for the benefit of the constituents. All parties are on the same team, they cooperate together to support the strategic plan and execute the operating plan. Employee labor and capital are in a cooperative relationship.

The twentieth century was an amazing one in the history of the world. In one hundred short years man's brilliant transportation and production inventions moved many societies from agrarian to industrial with great growth in wealth. Next computing and communication inventions moved many nations to compete on a global basis, again with great growth in wealth. On the other hand, in that same one hundred years governments were also corrupt, cruel, and inept. Revolution and abuse of power in government moved many nations to poverty and starvation.

Many American corporations have been successfully providing great products and services, a good return on capital and a growth experience for employees. The leaders developed management processes that enabled all levels in the organization to cooperate and grow the business. When you see a major corporation fail, it is because politicians interfered with free market capitalism and unions used politicians to stop the company's progress on the experience curve.

Now let us turn our attention to polarization and discuss what it will take to overcome these highly charged wedge issues.

CHAPTER**FOUR**

POLARIZATION

*Conquer and Oppress is a polarizing doctrine that left
81 percent of the world's population impoverished*

Scientists suggest that Planet Earth started to form, along with
our solar system, about 4.6 billion years ago. Over the next
800 million years the earth formed from gases and molten
materials. As cooling took place the earth changed from liquid to a solid globe with a liquid core. The crust was formed,
solid materials, such as rocks evolved, and erosion started. A
primitive bacterial life form appeared around 3.5 billion years
ago. Sometime between 2.5 and 1.8 billion years ago oxygen
appeared and over time killed off many bacterial life forms and
allowed multi-cellular life forms to evolve. This evolution to
plant life and animal life continued until 543 million years ago.
Then many plant, fish, bird, and mammal species continued to
develop until 65 million years ago.

From this period on to current times, there have been several periods of significant climate changes and other unknown events that caused certain species to become extinct and new species to be introduced. Even though modern archaeology, with improved techniques, has found an impressive fossil record that supports evolution, there have been no findings that demonstrate how the beginning of a new species evolved. A leap of faith is required to believe the new species evolved just as it is a leap of faith to believe the new species was created by a creator.

Ancestors of modern humans called Homo Sapiens-Sapiens appeared as a new species about 100,000 years ago. The period from 5,000 BC to present is known as the recorded period of human civilization. Languages were developed that could be written down and communicated in words and pictures. Bartering was developed to encourage trade and was improved by using precious metals or coins as a form of currency.

EVOLUTION AND RELIGION ARE POLARIZING IDEOLOGIES THAT CAN BE RECONCILED

Many people today have faith in the fossil record and the evolution theories of Darwin and others, and do not feel comfortable with a spiritual or religious basis for the origin of life. Such people, who consider themselves atheists, humanists, and materialists (the only thing that exists is matter), believe there is no god or creator. They support their belief with archaeological records, and the opinion of notable men, who believed all forms of life on Planet Earth evolved over time through a random process of natural selection. Survival of the fittest is the credo. Benjamin Wiker, a religious person, in his book *Moral Darwinism* lays out the secular case from Epicurus in 300 BC to Darwin and beyond. Such well-known individuals such as Gallileo, Newton, Darwin, and Nietsche, who considered themselves materialists, provide credible arguments for secularism.

Perhaps as many as 7,000 years ago, religious thought came to man in various forms. The Bible has become the basis for most Christian thought today. For the secularists the Bible is no more than a series of stories, fables, or myths that lay out a worthwhile moral doctrine. For others the Bible is the document that explains God's communication with man. Many believe that it is the word of God.

Today American's fall into three categories. There are those who believe strongly that there is no god or creator and prefer to keep religion out of all societal activities. Then there are those who are deeply religious and would prefer a society that attended church regularly and functioned in accordance with a moral code ordained by God. Thirdly there is a large middle ground of people who are unsure. Such people often consider themselves spiritual or religious and believe in a creator but are not comfortable with highly structured religious doctrines. The idea, from materialists, that there is no life after death makes most people uncomfortable. People in the middle ground do not believe they are the product of a random process of evolution, but prefer to believe the gaps in evolution are the result of an intelligent design by our creator.

It would appear on the surface that the scientific belief, there is no god, and the religious belief, there is a god, are incompatible. An interesting article *Genesis on the Origin of the Human Race* by Roy A. Clouser makes a case that resolves the conflict.

The fossil record shows remains of early man dating back over 200,000 years. The Bible shares stories starting with Adam and Eve that may go back 7,000 years. Homo Sapiens-Sapiens, the two-legged human species, started about 100,000 years ago, migrated around the world to different climates and evolved physically and mentally, according to Darwin, into the many ethnic characteristics we have today. Sometime during the last 7,000 years, God and man started to communicate effectively. God shared with man that he created man in his own likeness and if man followed God's teachings or moral code, then life on earth could be peaceful and prosperous. As man accepted God's word, he became a spiritual man.

Clearly as we review recorded history over the last 7,000 years, growth of the human race toward peace and prosperity has not been easy. In fact today the world is polarized between religious and nonreligious people with extremes in both camps.

As man became more intelligent and more spiritual he aspired to loftier goals for all of humankind. Unfortunately good results in building nations have rarely been achieved, because the leaders of our societies dominated the people by using the Conquer and Oppress philosophy, in direct conflict with human nature and the teachings of Jesus Christ. The human race practices survival of the fittest and is naturally very competitive.

This is a good quality for self-reliance, but is counter-productive when subjected to slavery or oppression. This is an inherently unstable proposition. The people become rebellious under the oppression of their leaders. Even well-meaning religious organizations have conquered and oppressed people to achieve their goals. In other words, the end justifies the means. Consequently power has ebbed and flowed between the elites in power and the impoverished, enslaved class. Polarization over religion remains a significant challenge to achieving peace and prosperity for all.

WHAT'S BEST FOR AMERICA, SELF-RELIANCE
OR THE NANNY STATE?

If individuals are motivated to grow every day and to learn new knowledge or skills that are useful for everyday living, they can eventually produce enough to cover their needs for food, clothing, and shelter. When this occurs depends on the encouragement provided. Some may be comfortable moving toward self-sufficiency in their teens while others develop different skills and are ready in their twenties. In any event, if each person continues to grow in ways that have high value in the marketplace, their personal productivity means they produce more than they need to live. The individual can invest this excess into education or in assets that generate income.

At this stage, with a stake in personal prosperity, each person becomes aware of the return on their work and strives to invest it wisely. To do this, they can become an independent contributor or work within a business or corporation. The person gets quick feedback on his skills by checking the results of the enterprise and his contribution. To be successful, the business must develop and deliver outstanding products to customers. Customers who need the products will pay for the product benefits.

Being a pragmatist, this self-motivated entrepreneurial individual realizes there are services he would like his government to perform. The government needs to make a minimum set of laws for the society to function well and to see that they are judicially followed. Because citizens would like to feel safe from outside attack, they are comfortable investing in a powerful military managed by the government. All these attributes are consistent with the American Constitution.

Finally, even with the bulk of financial challenges being taken care of locally with family, friends, and local charity, a minimum fund for unseen events would be considered appropriate for a modern society. Under no circumstances would a responsible, self-reliant person want his government to manage any other businesses.

For this government service, he is prepared to invest a reasonable amount. A responsible person would want to invest a fair share of his hard-earned money, even if he is only earning a small level of income above his self-sufficiency. He would realize that it is important for each person to have some skin in the game to have a stake in the results. He'd be appalled if his government suggested he was in too low of a class to pay taxes and would raise questions of questionable government service or corruption.

Prior to the nineteenth and twentieth centuries, dictatorships, monarchies, dynasties, imperialism, and colonialism, emboldened with Conquer and Oppress methods of growth, polarized the ruling and working classes. In the last two centuries, this sorry state of affairs was made even worse with government manifestos by Karl Marx leading to communism and socialism and *Mein Kampf* by Hitler leading to fascism.

Today, throughout the world, governments are mandating high taxes, social engineering handouts to welfare recipients to garner votes, and meddling in the free market. In many cases the people would prefer freedom from meddling that causes second-class citizenship. Polarization between government control and the desires of citizens is overwhelming. This issue can be framed by the following challenges: small government versus big government, individualism versus collectivism, egoism versus altruism, and conservative versus liberal.

America has demonstrated its superior society by becoming the strongest economy in human history. In addition we have a powerful military, the latest technology, and a constitution that provides the most freedom. On top of that, our people are very charitable. Amazingly these outstanding results have been achieved despite poor government leadership that has polarized people when it comes to the size and role of government.

UNIONS POLARIZE THE WORKFORCE AND BLOCK COMPANIES FROM USING THE EXPERIENCE CURVE FOR COMPETITIVE ADVANTAGE

Perhaps one can advocate that during the nineteenth century, as industrialization grew, unions improved the lot of workers in a few job categories. Unfortunately the tactics initiated by the unions, while improving life for their members in the short term, became counterproductive in the long term. Company owners and management had to learn that the Conquer and Oppress philosophy, entrenched for thousands of years, would not work in a global economy. By the mid-twentieth century it was apparent to many small and large companies that to compete effectively they needed a strategic plan that embraced customers, shareholders, and all employees in a symbiotic relationship.

The motivation, upward mobility, and retention of its employees became an important strategy to get everybody on the same team. Unions didn't understand this sea change and continued their counterproductive activities. Continuing old tactics of demanding higher pay and work rules for one or two jobs out of thousands of job descriptions locked their members into a lifetime of insecurity. Why? Because this higher pay and inflexibility eventually drives the enterprise out of business!

Instead all employees, including union members, should have been encouraged to learn, grow, and change and move up into better-paying jobs. Unfortunately union leaders led their members down the wrong path of strikes and threats. Perhaps a more enlightened company management, cooperating with a responsive union management, could have avoided the Detroit automobile manufacturer fiasco and better competed in a global economy.

Specific job descriptions may still have been outsourced as an important competitive strategy but company and union management would have encouraged the members to learn, grow, and change. Instead of waiting for union bosses to pressure politicians to increase the minimum wage and raise the benefits for the same job description, the members could have learned new skills and been promoted to higher paying jobs. Companies couldn't take advantage of the experience curve and compete effectively.

This polarization between management and worker is a significant problem worldwide and is an unproductive hangover from past practices. When power—government, corporate, and union management—becomes more important than the success of the people, then the people suffer.

AFTER TWO CENTURIES OF IMMIGRANT ASSIMILATION, OUR NATION IS NOW DIVIDED OVER WHETHER TO ASSIMILATE OR SEGREGATE

America, the greatest immigrant nation in history, has shown the way with outstanding results and performance. Full assimilation is best. It gets results. Our 230-year history also shows that it is not an easy path to take.

Prior to the Constitution in the seventeenth and eighteenth centuries immigration to North America was laissez faire. Mainly

Spanish pioneers came in the seventeenth century and French and English in the eighteenth century along with slaves from Africa and the Caribbean. The Europeans were often risk takers looking for a new opportunity to help build the colonies. By the time of the Declaration of Independence, over five million immigrants had arrived. Until 1875 the country was open to all immigrants who were considered citizens in transition. Immigration was not regulated although, shortly after the Constitution was signed, ship captains were required to keep a manifest of immigrants.

From 1875 to 1965 the federal government passed laws restricting certain groups. The Chinese were banned along with criminals, paupers, prostitutes, and other groups considered undesirable. This period considered those immigrants that were given legal permission to reside in the United States as under contract with some limitation regarding privileges. After five years they could apply for citizenship. Also during this period, after the 1920s, immigrants were limited by quota and by country.

From 1965 on, laws were passed that considered immigrants as affiliated to people already in the United States as part of a family unification program. In addition only a few green card immigration documents were issued for people with scarce job skills.

As I pointed out earlier, America grew its population at twice the rate of all other countries until the early 1900s. Because America assimilated these diverse groups into a patriotic country with one common language, the country grew GDP faster and greater than any other nation. How did this happen? History suggests America performed best when the borders were open and immigration unfettered, yet during this time there were many issues and challenges between second and third generation Americans and the new wave of immigrants. Government policy to control and influence has only slowed the population growth and provided mixed signals to immigrants that they are not welcome. Multiculturism, the latest politically correct movement, has only made groups antagonistic to each other.

I believe America was successful because the inherent human nature of survival of the fittest combined with an unfettered free market of ideas melded a growing population of diverse talents into a successful nation. First comes the opportunity—the Constitution communicated to people all over the world that a new country believed that all men are created equal and are given unalienable rights by their creator for life, liberty, and the pursuit of happiness. This paved the way for the American dream. If you worked hard and were industrious and virtuous, anything was possible. You could become healthy, wealthy, and wise and build a future for your family and your future generations.

Next comes the demand—Poor and persecuted people from around the world saw this as a golden opportunity, so they came and they persevered. When America said, "send us your poor your hungry your huddled masses," the flood gates opened and millions of immigrants wanted to become Americans.

Finally comes the assimilation—The first generation had many challenges: language skill level, and ethnic and cultural differences. Nevertheless they worked hard, many at more than one job. They were thrifty, they lived in poor conditions to save for the future, but above all, they instilled family values in their children and taught them that the American dream was possible, providing they learned, grew, and were prepared to change to succeed. This is where human nature, natural survival kicked in. Many of the first generation and most of the second generation did not have to be told to join with other immigrants and be assimilated into one nation under god. It came to them naturally. The people from the bottom up created this great nation by following the principles of the Constitution. Government policy should encourage immigrants to join the team and be proud to be an American. There is nothing more uplifting than singing "I'm proud to be an American" along with Lee Greenwood.

Today we have a different challenge. First we must control our borders by physical or technological means so we can know accurately who is in the country at any time and if they are here legally. After all this is the age of terrorism and there are quite a few people in other parts of the world who want to come to America to kill us. With today's technology, we should be able to accomplish this quite easily.

Second we want to convey to the rest of the world that we are an open society and it's easy to receive proper documentation in a short time to get in or out as long as we know who you are and what your purpose is. The world quota for people entering the country should be high and consistent with our strategic plan. There should be only four reasons or status for being physically in the United States: Visitor with a Visa, Student with a Visa, Immigrant with a Green Card, and Citizen with Citizenship Documents. The requirements for each category should be easy to understand and simply communicated.

Finally we must present to all comers a friendly open easy to get in attitude as long as we know who you are, why you are in the country, where you will be, and when you will be returning home. Visitors and students should be told if they do not leave when they have committed to, then they must get their change of plans approved. To encourage skillful people from other countries to seriously consider immigrating to the United States we must make them comfortable taking the risk to move themselves and or their families. We must realize how difficult it is to be assimilated and provide clear communication of this policy.

Perhaps a personal experience will illuminate the point. In the early 1970s my wife and I were living in Woodland Hills, California, and were reflecting upon the changes we had experienced living in America since 1960. Although we spoke in English, very similar to but not quite the same as the American version, we took a long time to feel completely comfortable in the culture. Initially we sought out other Brits where we could share common recollections, jokes etc. This lengthy time to get assimilated is not a reflection on American hospitality but says more about the experience curve newcomers must go through.

Today immigrants get very mixed signals from leadership and the press because America is divided on whether it welcomes newcomers. Those who promote multiculturalism believe that immigrants can stay with their own kind. Our country, along with many other nations, is polarized on whether to encourage immigration and how to assimilate the people. The bottom line is that America's leadership has compromised the successful immigration policy of the first 150 years and polarized the nation about immigration and assimilation.

WHAT'S BEST FOR PROSPERITY: SOCIALISM OR FREE MARKET CAPITALISM?

Earlier I pointed out that prosperity comes from the productivity of the individual. By producing the most valuable output possible, each person quickly supports his basic needs and then contributes excess output generating wealth for his own account. This wealth can be invested in education to further the skills of the individual or invested in assets that generate income or capital growth.

Early man bartered excess output with other similarly motivated individuals. This was an inefficient method of distribution so as time went on spoken and written languages evolved, along with a common currency for bartering goods and services. Gold or other precious metal coinage was used until paper money became effective for efficient trading.

As markets for certain products or services grew, individuals naturally evolved into small businesses and larger corporations. Often the capital for developing, producing, and distributing the small business's product was provided by one owner. As companies grew, management raised capital by selling shares of equity in the company to several private individuals. This is now known as a private placement. A regulated market also developed for very large companies where shares could be sold to millions of shareholders. This is considered a public market regulated today by the Securities and Exchange Commission (SEC).

This natural development of business to meet the needs of customers is called capitalism. Capitalism means the assets, and means of production and distribution, is owned by private individuals. In order to compete effectively under capitalism, supply, and demand dictate pricing, creating a free market.

Free market capitalism is considered today by most forward thinkers as the best way to improve the prosperity of everyone on the planet. There was a consensus supporting this thesis in western countries from 1800 to the First World War in 1914, creating over one hundred years with peaceful periods and prosperity.

Unfortunately many power-hungry leaders in the twentieth century used the manifesto of Karl Marx, and the old method of Conquer and Oppress, to justify revolution. This travesty led to communism dictatorships and socialism (pseudo democracies) where the state owns the means of production and distribution. Our current administration is following this same path to failure.

During the twentieth century there were over seventy wars or conflicts around the world. The end result was poverty, starvation, and millions of deaths. It should be clear to all the leaders of the over two hundred nations today that Conquer and Oppress does not work. Even in America, where the Constitution, the character of the people, and the acceptance of free market capitalism has prevailed, the elite leadership has stifled the potential of the country.

Let's move on to a discussion of natural competition to discover how we may lay these polarization challenges to rest.

CHAPTER FIVE

NATURAL COMPETITION

A proven principle that can show the way to stable markets

In the last chapter I discussed how the world is a polarized place. This chapter will unravel the nuances of natural competition so that we can see clearly the possibilities for prosperity and peace. A theory of natural competition, enhanced by strategic competition, will lead to segments, or market niches, of stable coexistence between competitors. Furthermore productive use of resources will benefit the people. As businesses and nations compete on a global basis trading products, people, and capital, shared knowledge will reduce the polarization.

We start with the individual who learns to grow and change so that he can compete with himself, his environment, and others for survival. Once surviving he can then produce more, investing the extra income in assets that generate wealth. This leads to competing in business as an individual or as part of a group or corporation. Understanding how natural competition in business benefits the individual leads to a discussion in the next chapter on the benefits of portfolios of business (modern conglomerates). Modern conglomerates are a useful model to develop nations that improve the wealth of all the people applying the *Compete and Empower* model.

NATURAL COMPETITION IS THE BASIS FOR SURVIVAL

To compete is nature's gift for improving all forms of life on earth in an environment that is forever changing. First we compete against ourselves. To learn, grow, and change every day empowers every one of us to survive and to prosper in environments that may be out of our control. When we rise to the challenge with peak personal performance, we discover that anything is possible.

Consider the young child who sees an Olympic athlete breaking records and learns the athlete's story of personal growth. This may empower the child to start his own journey. He will have different challenges and successes along the way, and may choose to take a different path to a different goal. When challenging oneself to learn, grow, and change, one should not be intimidated by a peer who may be getting better results at any point in time. Furthermore, the self-motivated person will resist any attempt by a peer to oppress, bully, or ridicule him. Better yet, he might empower disgruntled peers by sharing the joy and benefits of personal growth with them.

A secondary source of competition is other people. Because a lifetime journey takes many different roads, there are no absolutes for performance at a specific point in time. We should consider the other person's story as information about the competition, showing us what's working and what's not. We can then change our own resume to set us apart from the competition and help us achieve our objectives.

As we check our personal performance of today against yesterday's, last week's, or last year's, we should give ourselves an "Atta-boy" or "Atta-girl" so we'll continue to learn, grow, and change every day.

FREE MARKET COMPETITION

The free market comes from the needs and wants of all the people of the world. First people need to cover the basics of food and shelter. When a person can cover these basic needs for himself and his family and have time or assets available beyond basic needs, he starts to discover additional needs and wants that he believes will improve his life. Because people produce products and services to meet the needs of themselves and others, they are both producers and consumers. Over time the value of the products and services will depend on the importance to the consumer and to the balance of supply and demand.

Natural competition creates a wide range of competitors, from individuals, to small and to large businesses. Initially the primary market is described by end use or application. Food products are produced and sold to consumers to be eaten, clothing is produced to be worn, houses are produced to be lived in, and games are produced to be played and so on. Over time secondary markets develop for products that become useful to several groups of end-user applications. For example autos for transportation, computers for personal productivity, and accounting services to report taxes.

Markets are segmented naturally by location in addition to end-user application. Over time a successful producer could sell its products in several locations, providing transportation and energy cost was not an impediment. Ideally, as the consumer changes his expectations of products or services, and the producers change the features and benefits of the product accordingly, then we have an efficient free market. Everyone benefits from this approach. The consumers get what they want at the best prices, and the producer's shareholders get a good return on their investment, and the employees get a great place to work with many opportunities to grow. But when a local, regional, or national government intervenes in response to the complaints of a special interest lobby by applying a tariff or tax on certain products or services, the system ends up with winners and losers and a distorted, non-free market. Over time such intervention always fails.

EFFECTIVE COMPETITION

For an individual, small, or large business to effectively enter a market with a new product, it must honestly analyze itself by asking the following questions:

Is this a real opportunity with staying power?

- Is there a customer need or want?

- Can the customer buy?

- Will the customer buy?

- Does the business have a product concept?

- Can the product be developed?

- Will the product satisfy the market?

- Can the business win with this initiative?

- Does the product have benefits, features, and performance that significantly exceed the competition?

- Is the price or value competitive?

- Does the timing fit the need?

- Can the business compete in sales and marketing?

- Can the business compete in engineering and production?

- Does the business have management, assets, and financing to win long term?

Is the opportunity worth exploring?

- Is the market segment high growth?

- Can the business afford it?

- Is the return adequate?

- Is the risk acceptable?

- Does it provide good value for customers, shareholders, and employees?

The business must look carefully at its assets (land, facilities, equipment, and intellectual property), its ability to finance the working capital needs, and whether it has the people required to succeed. The business must assess all its needs to get to the desired market share within the competitive environment, be able to acquire what's needed over the long haul, and achieve a good return on discounted cash flow. The mistake often made is to waste cash. An inexperienced CEO might spend excess cash on wasteful projects that would not pass muster if they were scrutinized properly. A politician may increase taxes and not spend the money wisely. In any event for all the people or a nation to increase their wealth, excess cash cannot sit around with marginal returns. It must be invested for the best return possible. Otherwise people do not get wealthier.

CLARIFYING THE MARKET

Markets have four levels of maturity: the early adopters, the early majority, the late majority, and the laggards. Early adopters are customers that enjoy buying a new product immediately when it hits the market. According to Geoffrey A. Moore in *Crossing the Chasm,* the early adopters are considered the "low hanging fruit," and easy to win because they always buy the latest gadget.

After the initial rush, a chasm of sales growth appears between the early adopters and the early majority, because the sales process changes from an impulse buy to a return on investment (ROI) buy where the sale must be justified. The late majority are the hardest to sell. They want it proven that a purchase will be a good ROI and a safe bet. The laggards are the tail of the customer distribution that is not compelled to buy.

ENTERING A NEW MARKET

A company can choose to enter a market at any one of the four levels of maturity. The easiest level to enter is the early adopter stage because there is no clear competitive leader. Strategies and tactics are changing to determine the best customer experience until a leader emerges. The early majority stage presents more challenges to a new competitive entry because the first, second, and third competitive positions are forming and may already have been formed. At the late majority stage, the customers have most likely chosen their preferred competitor and the first, second, and third positions have stabilized into a 2-to-1 ratio. Number one is twice the size of number two and so on.

Perhaps the first choice is to enter the market at the early adopter level, which is characterized by high growth, speculative market size, debatable growth at maturity, uncertain product acceptance (customer satisfaction), and many competitors. This is a good market entry point because there is no clear leader at this time. Several competitors are marshaling their resources, evaluating the customer's needs, and analyzing the competitors. Early success will depend upon the strength of the product differentiation, how well the company fits the customer's needs, and how brilliant is the strategy.

As the market evolves, three or four competitors will move into the top positions. According to Bruce Henderson, this is when his first perspective, the experience curve, comes into play. The leader's superior strategy enables him to sell more products and grow faster. The leader's quality improves, and costs fall faster than it does for competitors in the second and third positions. All of the competitors are moving down the experience curve at different rates as their volumes increase. The leader gains a competitive advantage in lower cost and higher quality by taking advantage of the experience curve principle.

In time, Bruce Henderson's second perspective comes into play. As the market matures, the weaker competitors leave the market, the market stabilizes around three or four competitors (usually three), and the leader is twice as large as the number two competitor who is twice as large as the next. The profitability (ROI) is also highest for the leader and lower for the lower positions. At this point, with the leader at fifty percent market share, the number two competitor at 25 percent and the number three at 15 percent, the market is considered highly stable. The market continues to grow at an attractive rate, and each competitor learns to manage the customer experience and his asset use so that his financial performance is acceptable. The other competitors usually leave the market gracefully when it is clear they won't meet their investment goals.

Portraying a typical business cycle on a Relative Market-Share versus Market Growth Matrix can help to develop strategy at the differing levels of market maturity. When entering a market segment, it's best to look for high growth greater than 10 percent and preferably in the 25 percent to 100 percent range.

Relative Market Share Matrix

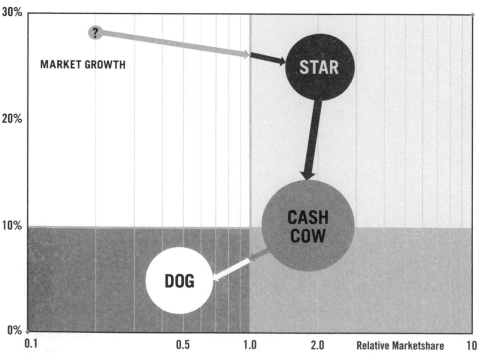

Investing in a new, high growth business is risky. If the new business starts out behind early competitors, then it belongs in the upper left hand quadrant of the Relative Market Share Matrix. This quadrant is characterized by high growth and less than 1.0 relative market share. We call this business a "question mark" or a start up.

If the strategy is sound and the execution exemplary, this new business emerges as the leader and moves into the upper right hand quadrant characterized by high growth and relative market share greater than 1.0. This means the business is now the biggest competitor. It is now considered a 'star' performer in growth and profitability. Usually because of the high growth rate and improving profitability, the "star" business will need cash to grow.

Over time, the overall market growth will slow down when most of the new customers have been satisfied and the market enters a maintenance level. With slower growth the business enters the lower right quadrant and becomes a "cash cow," a business that generates cash rather than consuming it.

Finally if the business is maintained but neglected, it enters the lower left quadrant of slow growth and low market share. We call this a "dog" that should be sold or liquidated.

ENTERING A MATURE MARKET

A more difficult alternative is to enter the market at the early majority or late majority levels. The risks of entry and the potential for success are similar in both cases because the competitors have already gone down the experience curve, but it may be more advantageous to enter at the early majority level if the market positions of the competitors have not yet stabilized.

Market shares can be changed in a relatively short time if a new competitor or an existing competitor challenges the status quo. Changing market shares is an expensive proposition for the aggressor. A new leader can grow to two times its nearest competitor providing it has the strategic intent to follow through and invest the necessary assets to survive the turbulence created during the unstable period. In order to be effective, the business had to believe it had enough competitive advantage to get a good return on the high level of cash invested throughout the time of changing market shares.

One approach for a new competitor entering a more mature market is to develop a strategy that enables the new competitor, over a realistic time frame, to become the new leader. This will take a very compelling product with an outrageous claim to get the attention of existing customers of the top three. If the overall market is growing rapidly, over 10 percent, the new competitor can quickly capture 10 percent market share by focusing on new customers. Additional market share is expensive to win because a satisfied client from one competitor must be wooed to the new player. Furthermore, if the market is large, the new competitor will need substantial financial resources to finance the working capital. In time, if this plan appears too formidable or risky, the new competitor's strategy should change. The new competitor readjusts its investment to become the number two or three player.

The essence and beauty of the natural competition perspective is that the marketplace reaches stability, where a few competitors co-exist in a peaceful, profitable environment that is difficult to shake up. It is still possible for a new competitor to shake up a market if the company has the strategic intent to do so but, the company will need to have the knowledge, people, and financial resources to stay the course. After a period of turbulence and uncertainty in the market, as competitors change market positions, the end result will again be an orderly stable market.

DEVELOPING A NEW MARKET SEGMENT

A completely different approach to enter a large, relatively stable, high-growth market is to create a new segment, thus avoiding direct confrontation with the well-established leaders.

A new competitor analyzes the customer's needs and determines that a small segment of the customers are not satisfied with the existing products and is looking for something new. This segment is often growing more rapidly than the overall market and offers an opportunity for new contenders. This market segment can look like a new business area with similar characteristics to the early adopter market discussed earlier.

A new segment of a mature market can be shown to have staying power by results from the first competitor. If customers are clamoring for the new and exciting product and the business is growing rapidly, then it is highly likely that this segment will grow into an exciting business. Early success and lots of publicity will attract other start up businesses or new teams in larger companies to look seriously at entering the new segment. A turbulent period will ensue based on the strategic intent of the competitors. Eventually the principles of natural competition will prevail. A leader will emerge, and the market segment will stabilize with three or four competitors.

So far we have discussed natural competition from the following perspectives:

1. Personal

2. New market

3. Mature market

4. New entry into a mature market

5. Developing a new segment in a mature market

The cell phone market provides a real-world example of developing a new segment in a mature market.

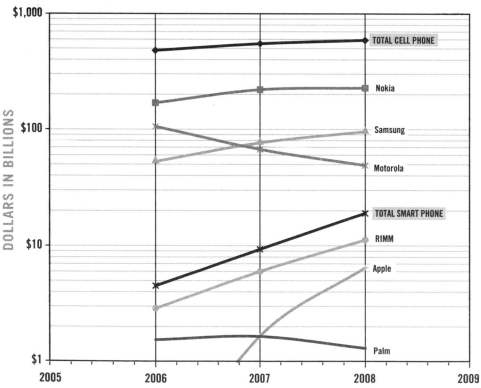

Cell Phone Market

The total market is over $500 billion and growing at less than 10 percent. Nokia is clearly the leader and twice as large as Samsung that holds the number two position. In a stable, mature market it would be rare to see a substantial shift in market share between Motorola and Samsung, but either Samsung had a vastly superior strategy or Motorola screwed up big time. Whether the market stabilizes around the 2008 positions depends on whether Motorola wants to re-group, mount a new strategy and investment and attempt to change the game. Smaller competitors such as LG and Sony will either leave the market or be satisfied with a low return in a specific region of the world.

By the second quarter, 2009, Motorola has continued to suffer from a weak strategy and has dropped below LG in market share. LG will most likely continue in the number 3 position

The smart phone new segment is very exciting, growing at over 100 percent per year. Palm defined this segment first with the TREO in the early 2000s. RIMM entered the market after Palm with a superior strategy. It targeted the corporate buyer and provided significant benefits and features that supported corporate security and the needs of the individual employee. RIMM is clearly the segment leader.

Along comes Apple with its superior touch and feel, aesthetics, and powerful software. Apple has shaken up the market and reduced Palm's position. The competition is not over. Only time will tell who finally wins and who settles for second and third positions. Eventually each competitor will consider its investment and how to get a reasonable ROI and will set its maturing strategy accordingly. Natural competition will play out, and the market will stabilize.

An early competitor, or a new one, may be empowered by the success of the leading competitors and decide to compete with a new strategy and resources. Early success is no prediction of future competitive advantage, just as current profitability is no guarantee that the total cash flow will be positive. Growth is no guarantee that continuing to invest will win in the end. Competing is not for the faint hearted but the end result is usually empowering for all concerned.

Natural competition enables competition to occur without bloodshed. The market is stable and peaceful, competitors have increased their wealth and prosperity, individuals have empowered themselves and others, and competitors have observed the results of others and been empowered to compete.

The end result of natural competition over time is a large, overall free market segmented into many market segments of all sizes. For the most part, there are only a few competitors in each segment and the markets are stable, peaceful, and profitable.

TWO BEHAVIORS THAT ARE COUNTERPRODUCTIVE

Let us now discuss two hypothetical situations and relate them to the cell phone industry to emphasize the point that Conquer and Oppress behaviors do not work.

First it should be said that all the competitors in the cell phone case are modern corporations where all the employees work together as a team to produce a great customer experience. They follow the principles of natural competition and are efficient at moving down the experience curve. In addition, they consider all their resources as valuable assets and over the mid and long term intend to get a good ROI.

The first hypothetical situation aids our understanding of union philosophy and its destructive results. What if Apple had decided to assemble its early units in the United States because it was underusing some local assembly resources? Then, a union had bribed politicians to approve the new card check initiative using union dues to fund re-election campaigns. With card check as backing, union operatives strong-armed the Apple assembly people to join the union. The union's next step would be to demand higher wages, higher benefits, and work rules to control the assembly operations. If Apple management conceded to such demands, they would not be able to compete because they would be stopped from going down the experience curve.

What if Apple's entry into the market was so successful that it asked its customers to rank the benefits and features they liked? What if the answer was "we love the touch and feel of the product," "we are thrilled with the power of the software," "we can really benefit from all the applications," and "we are indifferent to where the product is assembled"? Based on this feedback, Apple's strategy would be to outsource the assembly to Asia. The union response would be to lean on politicians to change the policies and rules to stop Apple's ability to assemble in Asia.

The mantra that is so destructive for prosperity is the quote, "save the jobs." If our parents and schools supported the self-reliance principle and taught our children to learn, grow, and change, then the assembly personnel would see this entry-level job as just a stepping stone to a more purposeful life. They would not join the union and rely on unprincipled organizations to keep them in the status quo for life.

The second hypothetical situation illuminates the failure of Conquer and Oppress leadership from the top. What if the Apple CEO had behaved like Hugo Chavez of Venezuela? First he would change the rules at Apple to dictate how funds are spent. He would then attack the CEO of Nokia and call him names and threaten him. Next he would set aside billions of valuable company cash to use in nefarious ways against Nokia. He would then visit fringe competitors in the cell phone market and attempt to bribe them with the extra cash confiscated from the corporate funds to also challenge Nokia. The end result of such crazy behavior would be to waste a lot of cash with no return, diminish the performance of Apple's most valuable asset, the people, and ruin the company.

If Hugo Chavez had learned from successful companies competing effectively with good returns, he would have taken into account his windfall cash from the oil market, the strength and capabilities of his people, and he would have found a profitable strategy to compete in a segment of the world market. With such a sensible strategy, he could have made Venezuela a more prosperous country for all its citizens.

BASIC BUSINESS TRUTHS THAT SUPPORT NATURAL COMPETITION

Analyzing results over our country's 230-year history, I have found, along with many companies I have mentored, that to operate a productive prosperous business it helps to follow certain principles. These eight basic principles have been shown to work in pursuing free market capitalism and both natural and strategic competition.

Basic Business Truths

1. **Accept that growth is essential for success ...** Customers get better products/services over time. Employees get an opportunity for a career with increasing compensation. Investors get a reliable return on investment.

2. **Recognize that taking a profit is like breathing ...**
    Without it, the company dies. With profit, investors
    get a good return. The business gets capital to improve
    productivity. The operation gets working capital to
    expand the business.

3. **Leading market share controls the market segment ...**
    Understand the total available market (TAM). Carefully
    define the served available market (SAM). Compete
    within resource capability until twice the size of the
    nearest competitor is achieved. When segment is stable,
    grow to sustain market share.

4. **Move aggressively down the experience curve ...**
    Instill total quality management (TQM) in all
    employees. Remove all road blocks to change.
    Expect significant productivity and quality gains.

5. **Invest resources in a few core competencies and
    outsource the rest ...** Develop core competency in
    resources that provide significant competitive advantage.
    Recognize that core competencies may change over
    time to remain competitive. Provide education and
    career paths for employees to change with the business.

6. **Plan strategically long term ...** Execute tactically short
    term. Prepare a six year or more strategic plan. Review
    annually in second quarter. Prepare an annual operating
    plan in fourth quarter. Execute to meet or exceed the
    operating plan but keep in mind the strategic mission
    and goals.

7. **Expand slowly behind the revenue growth ...** Strive
    for productivity improvements. Add resources only
    when essential and they can be managed effectively.

8. **Resize quickly ahead of a revenue downturn …**
   Reduce resources more than you think necessary.
   Motivate the remaining resources to win, and execute
   the revised plan. Support personnel reduction with aid
   to find a new opportunity in a growing company. This
   action will maintain a good reputation for doing the
   right thing when the company starts to hire again.

In this chapter, I introduced you to natural competition
and how we compete personally and through our businesses. By
developing businesses that encourage a symbiotic relationship
between customers, investors, and employees we get the beneficial result of increasing wealth for all concerned. In addition, if
the cash generated is quickly returned to profitable investments,
then wealth is further increased. In the next chapter, I will show
how further increases in wealth can be developed by combining
several successful businesses into a modern conglomerate. This
conglomerate model is applied to nations and provides a path
to peace and prosperity for all the people.

CHAPTER**SIX**

BUSINESS COMPETITION

Peaceful principles that can lift the spirit and the people out of poverty

In the last chapter we demonstrated that people can compete at the personal level and business level and do so peacefully. This competition divides the free market up into many small, medium, and large segments where a few competitors can coexist in each segment, grow, deliver a good customer experience, and provide a profitable performance for employees and shareholders. Other individuals and businesses will then be empowered by these successful enterprises to develop their own competing strategy, to find a market segment where they can compete effectively. I call this the *Compete and Empower* doctrine.

Let us now move on to understanding how companies can be organized into conglomerates and reduce their risk through diversification. Once we understand that this conglomerate business model is a more powerful version of *Compete and*

Empower, we can apply these principles to governments. Then nations can compete with each other without oppressing their people and threatening troop action to resolve national disputes.

Conglomerates use diversification strategies to expand into other business segments and different regions of the world and to operate businesses at different levels of maturity. With a good diversification strategy, growth is improved, risk is reduced, and the cost of capital is lower. With good leadership the financial markets value the whole enterprise higher than the individual pieces.

To compete effectively, nations must limit their government activities to supporting businesses, not running them. Government staff, steeped in strategic planning the BCG way, must honestly appraise their country's physical assets, their people strengths, and their financial wherewithal. National strategic plans must set goals for GDP growth and the key resources that support that growth. Nations with such an enlightened attitude will deliver increasing wealth and prosperity to all its citizens.

When people are polarized, progress to peace and prosperity is seriously impacted. Leaders, stuck in ideology are unable to pursue a pragmatic path to workable solutions. They impede the ability of the people and their businesses to grow the nation's GDP.

Nations must embrace *Compete and Empower* and give up Conquer and Oppress.

HOW IS WEALTH CREATED?

People earn wealth by applying themselves to tasks or projects that compensate them for their efforts. If they are at the beginning of their journey to learn, grow, and change, their basic skills will most likely have a low market value. As they develop skills in shorter supply, their efforts will provide much higher compensation.

Once a person has earned enough to cover the basics of food, clothing, and shelter, that person may invest her additional compensation in self-development. Or an individual may invest in assets that generate additional earnings. Clearly then, wealth is created when earning power grows and people make careful, prudent investments of time and earned capital. In order to do this, individuals must develop skills that enable them to produce highly desirable products or services.

Clearly a market, a place where goods and services can be bartered or exchanged for liquid currency, is essential for these early steps to create wealth. Once upon a time, when man roamed the earth and was free to choose location and environment, men, and women could apply their talents on their own behalf and consume their own effort in satisfying the basics of food, clothing, and shelter. Once man decided to produce more than the basics of life, then he was producing excess beyond the family needs. This excess must be compelling goods and services that are valuable to others in order to create wealth. The more compelling the product, the more likely the consumer will see value and purchase the offering.

If the business of producing these goods and services is owned by the people and they are committed to satisfying the needs and desires of all the people in the segment of the community, nation, or world they've selected, then the business will succeed. If the business is confiscated by the government and centrally controlled, then it is most likely to fail.

The first scenario is a free market funded by the people's capital and invested by them as a free choice. The second is a planned market, controlled centrally by government bureaucrats and funded by taxes confiscated unwillingly from the people.

The free market is made up of millions of businesses large, medium, or small competing in millions of market segments around the world. Some are mature and stable; some are young with competitors striving for success. Some will make good decisions and thrive; some will make bad decisions and fail. The market will ebb and flow depending on the free choice of the consumer and the creativity of the competitor to produce compelling products. Over time some companies will be hiring and some laying people off. The self-reliant individual will go with the flow and learn, grow, and change to improve his skills and wealth over time.

If the overall market is increasing its GDP faster than population growth, profits are growing, and the cash is reinvested quickly and wisely, then the wealth of the average citizen will increase. If the leaders and governments of the world's nations Conquer and Oppress their people by confiscating cash from the rightful owners to line their own pockets or feed their programs that get them re-elected, then the wealth of the average citizen will decline. A good government, a government of citizen politicians, a government that serves the best interests of all the people, will minimize its spending and only propose services that can show a good ROI.

It is easy to see how a free market can slowly get polluted when a career politician's interests to get re-elected are in conflict with the people's interests. In the normal ebb and flow of the market, a business in the politician's district is failing. Instead of encouraging the laid-off personnel to look for better opportunities in more successful businesses, he makes a speech about the down-trodden worker and how we must save the jobs. The politician then supports spending confiscated productive cash to prop up a failing enterprise in the hope it will get him votes in the next election. The result of this behavior is to reduce the wealth of the nation and the citizens and encourage individuals to fail instead of succeed. Pure free market capitalism unfettered from crony regulation is best for the nation and the citizen economically and morally.

HOW IS BUSINESS ORGANIZED TO CREATE WEALTH?

In the individual business, the owner has all the skills and the motivation to perform all the functions and duties that are required for a successful enterprise. The owner may be called on to provide all or some of the following: ideas, market development, product development, market introduction, sales, order processing, manufacturing, shipping, servicing, accounting, and legal documentation. This is called a functional organization where the chief executive is a general manger responsible for growth and profit and manages the functions required to operate the business. In some cases, the owner may hire staff but the owner will ultimately be responsible for the business's success or failure and the performance of the business functions. This is considered a small business.

A larger enterprise builds a successful business for the benefit of all its stakeholders: customers, shareholders, and employees. The corporate role is to buy and sell assets for the benefit of shareholders. The business role is to produce and distribute products or services for the benefit of customers; the management role is to plan and operate the business for the benefit of employees, and the staff role is to support the operating functions for efficiency and ensure compliance with external rules and regulations. The best business grows and changes to meet the needs of all its stakeholders and at the same time generate a healthy profit and return on investment while using all resources productively.

The medium-sized business, with a single product or service, is similar to the small business. It usually serves a single market segment and is organized functionally. If the medium-sized business is large enough, then the ownership maybe be distributed among many shareholders. A medium-sized business may grow large but stay in a single product business, and be organized functionally to create a great experience for a large customer base.

Medium, and large-sized businesses often organize themselves into multi-business enterprises. Such enterprises are sometimes called conglomerates. In this model, each business may be just a division of the overall corporation or they could be separate legal entities where all the shares are owned by the conglomerate corporation. The individual businesses could be small, medium, or large.

THE CONGLOMERATE BUSINESS MODEL

In a conglomerate's simplest form, each business is completely separate and controls all the assets it needs to operate successfully. Each business has a chief executive, a management team, and many employees from entry-level to top level. In a modern business, committed to competing effectively, all the employees function as a team and deliver annual results that meet or exceed the operating plan and five-year performance that achieves the strategic plan. The financial performance of the conglomerate corporation is determined by consolidating together all the financials from each business.

The chief executive officer (CEO) of the conglomerate corporation has an interesting strategic dilemma. How do the functions he staffs at the corporate level add value to the total enterprise? In other words, is the share value of the conglomerate higher than the sum of the value each business could get in the open free market? You can see this dilemma played out in the market every day. Great conglomerate CEOs like Warren Buffet generate shareholder value greater than market averages over the long haul and are heralded for their acumen. Others who perform poorly are heckled by their shareholders until the board removes them from office or until there is a takeover of the board and the conglomerate is sold in pieces for a higher overall value.

Early in the last century, before corporations understood the benefits of natural competition, conglomerate CEOs convinced Wall Street it was more efficient to centralize functions like purchasing, sales, branding, finance, and contract law. Little did they realize the unintended consequence of lost market share in their businesses. The businesses could not compete effectively because they could not make their own outsourcing decisions and had to compete for resources at the trough of the centralized functions. Eventually this matrix organization fell into disgrace and, in many cases, was abandoned.

As they learned about natural competition, some conglomerate CEOs formulated a good strategy to support the businesses:

- Ask the business CEOs: "What do you need to be #1 or #2 in your business?"

- "If I centralize certain functions, will it affect your business?"

- Set high-performance goals with excess cash returned to corporate in conjunction with the business CEO.

- Support the business CEOs responses and plan.

- Hold the business CEO accountable to meet or exceed plan.

The conglomerate CEO also realized that the following strategy would add value and get the best results:

- Keep conglomerate corporate spending low, in the 1 percent to 5 percent range.

- Allocate and raise cash to get the lowest cost of capital: Acquire and develop a diversified portfolio of businesses to get great growth at minimum risk. Invest in a few start ups. Add as many star businesses as possible. Keep several cash cows to reduce the cost of capital.

- Create good relationships with the financial community.

- Interface with external agencies to minimize governmental (SEC), regulatory agencies, become expert in tax law, become expert in financial reporting.

- Minimize advertising and public relations at the conglomerate corporate level but get the message out.

Berkshire Hathaway, with Warren Buffet at the helm, is probably the best-run and most famous conglomerate of all time. He is a brilliant executor of the "Graham School" of value investing. He invests for the long term in minority positions in public companies that he understands. If offered 100 percent ownership of a business, he uses guidelines that involve purchase price, intrinsic value, and a desire for strong management to remain at the helm of the business being sold. Companies like Sees Candy, Helzberg Jewelers, and Geico Insurance are typical of those Berkshire owns outright.

A conglomerate I have concerns about is General Electric (GE). The company performed superbly under Jack Welch's leadership for twenty years. Welch had a demanding management style but encouraged the businesses to follow the natural competition principles. In order to get the overall performance, he must have managed corporate cash prudently. Since the turn of the century GE has a new CEO. The performance is deteriorating, and the stock value shows it. Instead of using corporate cash wisely, it seems the new CEO's strategy is to gamble the future on the whims of politicians. He is supporting the new green energy program and the new government run healthcare program and is on at least one presidential council. Using corporate cash to influence politicians can ruin a company because it is very hard to predict or control the outcome of this investment.

A GOVERNMENT BUSINESS MODEL
SIMILAR TO THE CONGLOMERATE

The government that understands natural competition should formulate a good strategy to support businesses:

- Ask businesses and business councils by industry: "What do your companies need to be #1 or #2 in their business?"

- "If the government centralizes or regulates certain functions, will it affect their businesses and how?"

- Collaborate with business leaders, and encourage business goals of high-performance with excess cash re-invested for GDP growth.

- Support the business and business council's responses and plans.

- Shareholders must hold the business CEOs accountable to meet or exceed plans.

The skillful government leader also realizes that the nation should follow these strategies:

- Keep government spending low (1 percent to 5 percent).

- Expect business leaders to manage cash flow for best return and lowest cost of capital.

- Reduce government regulations to minimize interference: SEC and other regulatory agencies.

- Enact the "Fair Tax," become expert in minimum financial reporting, and eliminate corporate tax.

- Encourage the commerce department to provide outstanding strategic plans and guidance that encourage GDP growth as the highest priority.

- Accept term limits to one eight-year term to save billions by not needing to be re-elected.

Clearly America and world leaders are a long way from the model of a smart conglomerate headquarter's staff. As we have pointed out earlier, all societies have been dominated by governments that believed in the Conquer and Oppress philosophy. Furthermore until the discovery of natural competition in the early 1960s most if not all businesses were run by the same methods. Management versus the workers!

HOW DID THE WORLD WANDER INTO THE WILDERNESS?

The road to failure was taken when man chose to compete by conquering and oppressing others. It is a self-defeating cycle of madness that continues today.

We have shown that natural competition for survival leads to a free market that empowers individuals and others. Because man had the freedom to choose, some individuals gained more wealth than others. Instead of accepting that the outcome was based on a free choice and that a person's choice was to be respected, some individuals decided they were better than their fellow man. A question that is difficult to answer is, "Are these individuals following a natural, survival, appropriate choice or by believing themselves better are they practicing sinful, deviant, and evil behavior?"

Either way, this attitude had devastating consequences. The elites enslaved the underclass and made decisions that manipulated the free market and sentenced millions to death or impoverishment. Such a world exists today where most, if not all, of over six billion people are governed by elitists who think they know what's best for the people. Even America, with all its success and a constitution that puts the people in charge, has been conned into accepting that the elites, the career politicians, are in charge.

The cycle of madness starts when a member of a tribe claims that he should be declared chief. The tribe appeases this barnyard bully by accepting his dictatorial behavior. The chief then adds supporters so that he can declare himself the monarch. The monarch then enslaves his people and conquers other tribes, killing the leaders and enslaving more people. Monarchs extend their reign by becoming dynasties. This cycle of oppression continues as monarchs compete by conquering other societies, such as Indians in the Americas and blacks in Africa, to provide cheap labor and confiscate any wealth embedded in the land.

There were a few extended periods where such societies appeared to work. A gifted leader would do the right thing for the people and a sense of success and prosperity prevailed. But when conditions change and the society fails to live up to expectations, the people rise up, revolt against the leadership, and install a different set of elites. The cycle of madness continues. This is the story of the twentieth century when the world experimented with communism, socialism, and dictatorships.

Think what a wonderful world we would live in today if civilization had evolved with a *Compete and Empower* doctrine. The prosperity of nations would have kept pace with the invention and entrepreneurship created by the individuals in our societies.

THERE IS HOPE FOR A BETTER FUTURE ON THE HORIZON

Today, because of the groundbreaking innovation that comes from natural competition and the refreshing attributes of globalization, free market capitalism provides the best path to prosperity. I believe that America's people and businesses have, for the most part over the last sixty years operated lawfully, successfully, and with integrity. There are always a few bad apples that break the law, but they should be brought to justice by our judicial system. The majority of business leaders act with integrity, honesty, and professionalism for the benefit of all the people—customers, investors, and employees alike.

On the other hand, our government has become both corrupt and incompetent. Who do you trust more, a business executive who shares his vision and strategy for the company with all employees, or the politician who becomes compromised by his career objectives, minority interests, and Washington lobbyists?

Today a business cannot succeed without following the *Compete and Empower* doctrine using the latest communication technologies. Share the company's vision and strategy, open up a global free market, gain knowledge with Internet communication, and participate in open-source movements like Wikinomics and social and business networks like YouTube, Facebook, LinkedIn, and Plaxo.

LET'S EXAMINE THE 2008–2009 ECONOMIC CRISIS TO HIGHLIGHT DIFFERENCES IN DOCTRINE

The End of *American Capitalism* by Anthony Faiola appeared in the *Washington Post* on October 10, 2008. Its opening gambit was, "The worst financial crises since the Great Depression is claiming another casualty; American-style Capitalism."

I disagree! Free market capitalism is not the problem.

The primary cause of the current financial crisis is interference in the free market system by politicians from both parties.

Not only does the Federal Reserve interfere with the market but the politicians keep changing laws like the "Community Reinvestment Act of 1977" to fit their political agenda. This act was started under the Carter administration to get banks to lend to minorities and was reinforced under the Clinton administration. Along the way, community activist organizations badgered the banks to persuade them to make loans that were not appropriate. Read *Meltdown* by Thomas E. Woods Jr. to get a fresh and helpful perspective and *Catastrophe* by Dick Morris to get the inside scoop.

The changes in the law enabled some banks and Wall Street companies to take on additional leverage/risk within the law. Pushed by the politicians and seduced by the changes in the law, some banks did not see, or chose not to see, the unintended consequences and changed their lending practices to meet the letter of new laws.

Over a twenty-year period, central control of the Federal Reserve and out-of-control politicians have allowed too much leverage and risk in the system. Panic set in when Lehman Brothers collapsed and the last administration's treasury secretary asked Congress to approve a $700 billion rescue package called TARP. Because American-style capitalism is being questioned, let us review the current crisis from the perspective of results accomplished.

During most of the twentieth century, our government and politicians have systematically manipulated the political process to take control of the government and to oppress the people with excessive laws, taxes, and regulations. For many years, the progressive liberals have attempted to follow the European Communist, Socialist philosophy. Thank God for the courage and character of the American people and their businesses, for the support of a Constitution that emphasizes liberty, and freedom, and free market capitalism. Because of this, America has grown its GDP to more than $14 trillion, over three times larger than any other nation.

America's Founding Fathers envisioned a country where the people were free to learn, grow, and prosper and the government was expected to serve and protect the people. They intended this representative government to be small and run by civilian politicians, not career politicians. Over the first 125 years, until the beginning of the twentieth century, federal government spending increased to about 1 percent of GDP. In 2009, spending is likely to be over 30 percent of GDP.

A majority of the people support a strong defense against both external and internal threats. About 5 percent of GDP is considered affordable and appropriate by most of us to protect our citizens. Robert Higgs, senior fellow of the Independent Institute suggests eight percent would better protect Americans in this dangerous world.

The rest of government is an overhead or drag on the productive output of the people. If we use modern American conglomerate corporations as an example, we would conclude that government overhead should be in the 1–6 percent range. I believe that our government should not spend more than 11 percent of GDP, 5 percent on defense, 5 percent on overhead, and 1 percent on safety net reserves.

What has gone wrong?

First, we must recognize that the only wealth and prosperity comes from the 125 million working Americans, self-reliant people free to innovate, develop, and produce products and services. These citizens operate individually or as part of a business team to produce the products and services for the 300 million, total population, to consume. Additional prosperity comes from exporting similar products to the rest of the world. In order to have free open trade, we also purchase imports from other countries.

From the 100 million people who earn enough to save and invest, the government confiscates taxes to pay for defense, government overhead, Social Security and Medicare. With the remainder, the employees support their families, their lifestyles, and their futures.

The remainder money invested by the 100 million people is the *only source of capital* available to businesses to grow and develop new products and markets. The American people have innovated, worked hard, shown strong character, taken entrepreneurial risks, and been empowered by the Constitution with its principles of liberty and freedom. Today, thanks to the people's efforts, America leads the world in GDP, prosperity, military strength, freedom, and charity.

Second, we must recognize that our elected representatives have impeded the people's ability to achieve even greater results. Federal taxes were increased to unhealthy levels on the individual's productive capital, which meant that capital was no longer available to free enterprise businesses, and the taxes were passed to the states for low return programs that supported re-election of the politician. During the Great Depression of the 1930s the economy stagnated for at least ten years because taxes were raised to excessive levels and spent on government make work programs.

During WWII most production focused on the war effort, but with the return of our victorious military and a shift to consumer production, an economic boom began.

Politicians realized they could use the tax code, government spending, and changes in the law to keep themselves in office. Suddenly their career goals came in conflict with what's best for America. The career politician was born.

It became popular to bash the businesses that generated jobs, growth, and prosperity, and to convince people they were second-class citizens, down-trodden workers, and victims of the wealthy. The politicians supported unions to emphasize this theme.

Unions are bad for business because they interrupt the experience curve and cause companies to fail. Businesses are good for the people because they provide job and income growth opportunities. Unfortunately this behavior by politicians started a cycle of corruption and oppression that still continues.

Where are we today?

We still have a very creative and industrious population impeded by the government. A consequence of the government's class warfare rhetoric is that an ever-increasing segment of the population has been indoctrinated to expect handouts. We also now have an out-of-control government that spends more and more without accountability.

Perhaps the most important concern for "we, the people" is that this political process has led to one set of rules for the people and their businesses, and another set for the politicians. Over the year's politicians, pandering for votes, have passed more and more regulations to protect the little guy, but do not follow the same procedures to approve their own spending programs.

Here's an example. Let us consider how a prudent business team growing a $10 billion business operates today. The company will have a strategic plan looking out five years and a one-year operating plan. It will make sure it has enough cash to meet plan at a reasonable cost of capital. If business is good, the company may need to raise working capital or development funds for growth. If business is bad, it may need to raise funds to deleverage the balance sheet and to carry on with an important program.

In any event, the company must be on top of the market and business circumstances because if it needs to raise money, it'll need to follow the laws set up by the politicians and take at least four to nine months to get it done. After careful consideration with management and key employees, the business decides to raise $1 billion.

Here are the steps the business must go through to raise money from the 100 million investors.

1. Consult with an investment banker who will advise the company of changes it must make to the company to have a successful financing. (One month)

2. Decide to make the changes and prepare for a public offering. (One month)

3. Inform the SEC of the Company's financing objective and prepare a public offering document in conjunction with corporate attorneys and investment banker personnel. This may require several iterations to get SEC approval. This is a legal quiet period with no company PR allowed. (Two to six months)

4. Get with an investment banker, and plan and execute a road show so the investment banker can test the valuation of the offering with his brokers. (one month)

5. Finalize the price (value), print the Offering Document, go public, and raise the funds. (Three days)

6. Total elapsed time four to nine months.

Here are the steps the politician goes through to raise money from the same 100 million investors.

1. Make a campaign promise that sounds good and will get votes (e.g., $700 billion for energy independence).

2. When elected, declare a crisis created by prior administration.

3. Under the mantle of a crisis, propose emergency funding to Congress that must be voted on immediately.

4. Rely on partisan leadership in House and Senate to prepare a bill.

5. Bring the bill to a vote before politicians can read and debate the bill.

Remember that the source of funds is the same for both the public offering of $1 billion above and the taxes to pay for the $700 billion proposal by politicians. The 100 million investors are the only source unless the politician borrows funds from foreign investors or prints the money.

Why is there one set of rules for politicians and a second set for the people's business? The difference in documentation and due diligence to attract investment capital of $1 billion versus government's approach to confiscate $700 billion in taxpayer funds from the same 100 million people is incomprehensible. How did the American people allow a few thousand public servants take over our country, stop following the Constitution, and steal our liberty?

I have introduced you to the benefits of natural competition and *Compete and Empower.* I have also shown you the destruction of civilized society that comes from allowing Conquer and Oppress to creep back into the government process. I will lay out a plan in Chapter 8 and a call to action in Chapter 9 that offer a solution to the challenges that face us. In the meantime, let's explore current examples of how the course of history could be changed by selecting suitable segments of the world market and strategically support our businesses to enter them through natural competition methods.

SUGGESTIONS ON EMPOWERING NATIONS TO COMPETE STRATEGICALLY

The U.S. State Department's mission in its 2007 to 2012 Strategic Plan is:

*"Advance freedom for the benefit of the American people
and the international community by helping to
build and sustain a more democratic, secure,
and prosperous world composed of well-governed states
that respond to the needs of their people,
reduce widespread poverty, and act responsibly
within the international system."*

In 2008 the State Department's budget was approximately $35 billion; $12.7 billion went to the State Department and $22.3 billion was foreign aid administered by the department.

Without getting into whether the State Department should be spending this amount of taxpayer money and whether using these funds for foreign aid is constitutional, let me suggest some policy changes that would benefit nations open to new ideas.

Re-direct a small portion of the $6 billion "Bilateral Development Assistance" budget to set up a powerful team of expert American consultants on strategic planning whose mission will be to train in-country personnel to compete successfully in high growth market segments. Let's call this new program SPOT for Strategic Planning Outreach Team.

The in-country *Strategy Team* of the host nation, with support from the American experts (SPOT), will recommend changes to host nation government policy that support local entrepreneurs and encourage businesses to invest in new growth market segments. *Compete and Empower,* zones similar to enterprise zones, would be established.

The *Strategy Team,* with participation from local business and government personnel, will do the following:

- Review the nation's GDP, growth rate, population, and productivity results over a five-year period.

- Compare the results to other nations in the neighborhood.

- Break the total market for their nation's goods and services down into segments.

- Analyze the competition and where the nation's businesses stand in market share.

- Observe whether the market competition is local, regional, or global.

- Determine market entry strategies most likely to succeed.

- Analyze how valuable the market segment is and the job skills required to win.

- Develop investment ideas where new "star" businesses can be created.

- Make sure the new opportunities can be funded by local private business.

- Make sure the business opportunity is sound enough to attract the right people skills, intellectual property transfer with technology alliances, and funding from global financial investors.

What is the U.S. government doing instead? The current approach to lend a helping hand and to meet objectives that fit America's self-interest is to provide funds to the government of the nation selected. The funds are administered through a program called "Economic Aid supporting U.S. Political and Security Objectives." This program should be redesigned to become an investment program rather than a spending program where the funds are not tracked and are often used to prop up a corrupt government.

After the *Strategy Team* has developed changes to its government's policy in support of *Compete and Empower* and the host nation's business community has created strategic growth plans, then professional venture fund people working for the American foreign aid program should consider making an investment. They may choose to be the lead venture investor or invest alongside other global venture investors. The benefit of this approach is that the American taxpayer funds will be invested professionally and will have an opportunity to make a significant ROI based on venture investing risk/return parameters.

With this new approach to foreign aid, let us review several groupings of nations, observe their current state of affairs, and suggest some possibilities on how *Compete and Empower* can make a big difference.

THE TWENTY FIRST-CENTURY CONTENDERS FOR WORLD LEADERSHIP

The following six nations are discussed most often by world experts as the nations most likely to succeed and lead the world. America, Japan, and China currently have the largest GDP. There are other western European nations with higher GDPs than Brazil, Russia, and India but because of their socialized governments they are not expected to achieve high growth.

Nations Competing for World Leadership

AMERICA	2000	2001	2002	2003	2004	2005	2006	2007	2008
GDP ($B)	$11,093	$11,176	$11,355	$11,640	$12,064	$12,433	$12,791	$13,050	$13,220
GROWTH (%)	3.7%	0.8%	1.6%	2.5%	3.6%	3.1%	2.9%	2.0%	1.3%
POPULATION (M)	282.3	285.0	287.7	290.3	293.0	295.7	298.4	301.1	303.8
PRODUCTIVITY ($)	$39,290	$39,212	$39,472	$40,091	$41,170	$42,042	$42,859	$43,337	$43,512

JAPAN	2000	2001	2002	2003	2004	2005	2006	2007	2008
GDP ($B)	$4,018	$4,025	$4,035	$4,094	$4,205	$4,284	$4,379	$4,468	$4,486
GROWTH (%)	2.8%	0.2%	0.3%	1.5%	2.7%	1.9%	2.2%	2.0%	0.4%
POPULATION (M)	126.7	127.0	127.2	127.4	127.5	127.5	127.5	127.4	127.3
PRODUCTIVITY ($)	$31,708	$31,697	$31,726	$32,147	$32,989	$33,591	$34,340	$35,060	$35,241

CHINA	2000	2001	2002	2003	2004	2005	2006	2007	2008
GDP ($B)	$1,456	$1,577	$1,720	$1,893	$2,084	$2,300	$2,567	$2,860	$3,126
GROWTH (%)	8.4%	8.3%	9.1%	10.0%	10.1%	10.4%	11.6%	11.4%	9.3%
POPULATION (M)	1,268.9	1,276.9	1,284.3	1,291.5	1,298.8	1,306.3	1,314.0	1,321.9	1,330.0
PRODUCTIVITY ($)	$1,148	$1,235	$1,340	$1,465	$1,604	$1,761	$1,954	$2,163	$2,350

BRAZIL	2000	2001	2002	2003	2004	2005	2006	2007	2008
GDP ($B)	$856	$868	$891	$901	$952	$980	$1,016	$1,072	$1,126
GROWTH (%)	4.3%	1.3%	2.6%	1.2%	5.7%	2.9%	3.7%	5.4%	5.1%
POPULATION (M)	176.3	178.9	181.4	184.0	186.5	189.0	191.5	193.9	196.3
PRODUCTIVITY ($)	$4,856	$4,851	$4,909	$4,897	$5,107	$5,187	$5,309	$5,526	$5,736

RUSSIA	2000	2001	2002	2003	2004	2005	2006	2007	2008
GDP ($B)	$590	$620	$649	$697	$747	$794	$853	$922	$950
GROWTH (%)	10.0%	5.1%	4.7%	7.3%	7.1%	6.4%	7.4%	8.1%	3.0%
POPULATION (M)	146.7	146.0	145.2	144.3	143.5	142.8	142.1	141.4	140.7
PRODUCTIVITY ($)	$4,019	$4,244	$4,471	$4,828	$5,202	$5,561	$6,003	$6,521	$6,749

INDIA	2000	2001	2002	2003	2004	2005	2006	2007	2008
GDP ($B)	$550	$578	$602	$654	$699	$758	$831	$906	$974
GROWTH (%)	3.9%	5.2%	4.1%	8.6%	6.9%	8.4%	9.7%	9.0%	7.5%
POPULATION (M)	1,004.1	1,022.0	1,039.7	1,057.5	1,075.5	1,093.6	1,111.7	1,129.9	1,148.0
PRODUCTIVITY ($)	$548	$566	$579	$618	$650	$693	$748	$802	$849

An important assumption for the following discussion is that world GDP growth should, on average, be 5 percent or greater because of the growing influence of global corporations steeped in natural competition strategy and the computer/communication technology revolution.

Clearly America stands head and shoulders above all others. The miracle of the American Constitution, coupled with the dynamism of a virtuous, courageous people and a commitment to free market capitalism over the last one hundred years, has delivered over a $14 trillion GDP economy. This wealth is at least three times the size of Japan, its nearest competitor. Since the 1960s America's growth kept up with the world growth rate and therefore retained its market share at about 28 percent. Unfortunately during the last decade America has grown at less than 5 percent per year, and is starting to lose market share.

China has achieved very good performance over the last twenty-five years. Ever since Deng Xiaoping released the entrepreneurial spirit of its people and made GDP growth through free market capitalism its highest strategic priority, China has grown on average 9.5 percent per year, almost twice the world GDP rate. China's market share has grown from less than 1 percent to over 7 percent. Current expert opinion is that China will continue to grow at 9 percent until it overtakes America around 2035.

The main reason the experts believe this will happen is that our leadership has moved America away from its Constitution and toward socialism similar to what's practiced in Western Europe. The current administration is accelerating this process under the guise of solving the current financial crisis. In addition the experts do not expect America to change its immigration policy back to pre-1965 days. Therefore America will not have grown and assimilated the workforce needed to support a $100 trillion GDP in 2050. They expect America to continue to lose market share as China overtakes us. China has the population to support a $60 to $100 trillion GDP by 2050 because people will migrate from the farms to new urban centers where their children will join the new talented, driven Chuppies (China Yuppie) population.

The world will be a better place if, through *Compete and Empower,* America and China establish themselves as America #1 and China #2 competing peacefully in a stable natural competitive segment. We will show you in Chapters 8 and 9 what America must do to make this happen.

What about the other players in this grouping? It is too early to tell who will become #3 or #4. Japan shows no sign of changing its strategy and focusing on GDP growth. Brazil is in a region of political unrest and has not demonstrated a strong conviction to transform its government to one that truly supports *Compete and Empower.* Russia has not developed institutions of integrity and continues to operate from a Conquer and Oppress philosophy. Perhaps India has the best possibility, with a large population that can be encouraged to learn, grow, and change and with signs of high growth, but it will need to shed off its bureaucracy and become more dynamic.

CAN *COMPETE AND EMPOWER* MOVE THE MIDDLE EAST TOWARD PEACE?

The following group does not show all the players in the Middle East, and there is no data on the Palestinians because they are not yet a nation, but we can consider some possibilities through the eyes of natural competition. The data for this group is powerful because it highlights the stark differences between Conquer and Oppress and *Compete and Empower.*

Some Nations Competing in Middle East

SAUDI ARABIA	2000	2001	2002	2003	2004	2005	2006	2007	2008
GDP ($B)	$255	$256	$257	$276	$291	$310	$323	$334	$357
GROWTH (%)	4.7%	0.5%	0.1%	7.7%	5.2%	6.6%	4.3%	3.4%	6.8%
POPULATION (M)	23.1	23.8	24.5	25.1	25.8	26.4	27.0	27.6	28.1
PRODUCTIVITY ($)	$11,014	$10,760	$10,480	$10,989	$11,278	$11,735	$11,966	$12,112	$12,683

ISRAEL	2000	2001	2002	2003	2004	2005	2006	2007	2008
GDP ($B)	$113	$113	$111	$113	$118	$124	$131	$138	$143
GROWTH (%)	7.6%	-0.3%	-1.2%	1.7%	4.4%	5.2%	5.2%	5.4%	3.7%
POPULATION (M)	6.1	6.3	6.4	6.5	6.6	6.7	6.9	7.0	7.1
PRODUCTIVITY ($)	$18,465	$18,015	$17,469	$17,435	$17,863	$18,442	$19,052	$19,722	$20,100

IRAN	2000	2001	2002	2003	2004	2005	2006	2007	2008
GDP ($B)	$39	$40	$44	$46	$49	$51	$54	$58	$61
GROWTH (%)	3.5%	3.4%	8.9%	5.0%	5.6%	5.6%	5.8%	6.6%	5.8%
POPULATION (M)	63.3	63.8	63.9	64.0	64.3	64.7	65.0	65.4	65.9
PRODUCTIVITY ($)	$614	$630	$684	$718	$754	$792	$834	$884	$929

SYRIA	2000	2001	2002	2003	2004	2005	2006	2007	2008
GDP ($B)	$22	$24	$25	$25	$26	$27	$28	$30	$32
GROWTH (%)	0.6%	5.1%	5.9%	1.1%	2.0%	3.5%	5.1%	6.6%	6.0%
POPULATION (M)	16.3	16.7	17.2	17.6	18.0	18.4	18.9	19.3	19.7
PRODUCTIVITY ($)	$1,373	$1,407	$1,453	$1,433	$1,427	$1,442	$1,481	$1,543	$1,600

This group is not a market segment but does indicate some of the difficulties of living in this neighborhood. Israel is a democracy and has competed effectively in high-technology market segments. It has a good reputation for its products and for satisfying its customers. With only 7 million people, it produces a GDP of $143 billion. I would have expected that its productivity at $20,000 per person would have been double that. Unfortunately several of Israel's neighbors are trying to annihilate it. The struggle to stay alive reduces the country's productivity. Even foreign aid and American support for a peace plan have been unable to solve the problem.

Saudi Arabia has a GDP twice the size of Israel, with a productivity of $13,000 per person (just above the poverty line) from a population of twenty eight million. Saudi Arabia operates in the OPEC market segment where competitors drill and extract oil and gas to sell on the world market. Instead of using the cash from the exploitation of their natural resources and investing it in new market segments empowering their people to learn, grow, and change the Saudi Arabian elites make passive investments on stock exchanges around the world. The country operates as a kingdom, where its wealthy king and other family members oppress its people. Saudi Arabia is, in reality, a form of dictatorship where the dictator has established a sense of stability by being friendly with America and Western Europe and providing just enough wealth to the serfs that they do not revolt. It is a balancing act that could topple at any time. Think how great it could have been if the king and his courtiers had the wisdom to use the natural resources and capital in conjunction with empowering the people to add value and grow GDP at much higher rates. Such wisdom would have made all the citizens wealthier and created a country that could be a beacon of progress like Taiwan, South Korea, and Kuwait.

Syria is also a pseudo dictatorship that oppresses its people. Unfortunately it does not have the natural resource wealth of Saudi Arabia so it keeps its citizens in poverty. In 2008 the people were barely surviving on $1,600 per person, way below the $10,000 poverty level. The elites keep company with terrorists and teach their people to hate and kill innocent people under the guise of a fringe element of the Muslim religion.

Iran is a much larger country than Syria with a population of 66 million people. thirty years ago, there was a revolution by the people. They installed mullahs, religious clerics, as their new dictators, who have since impoverished the people. The people exist on less than $1,000 per person per year. In the meantime, the elites have invested their cash unwisely in nuclear energy believing they can threaten their way to success by challenging America and Western European nations to a duel.

Time and again "tin pot tyrants," or today "oil barrel bullies," have taken on causes they cannot possibly win. Yet they get close because of appeasement from the powerful. I would like to see America try one more time to encourage these rogue nations to embrace *Compete and Empower.* To do this, we need to terminate America's current diplomatic initiative. It is unfair to blame America for many of the world's sorry state of affairs. It is embarrassing to be bowing to kings, and it shows a weakness that puts us at a disadvantage. America needs to stand proud of its contributions to mankind and to be willing, one more time, to share its knowledge of how to achieve prosperity for the people. Persuade these recalcitrant countries to let us send in our best strategic planning outreach team whose mission will be to convince them that their best interests will be served by transforming their nation to *Compete and Empower.*

THE CARIBBEAN COULD BE A TROPICAL PARADISE

In some ways, the Caribbean is already a tropical paradise. You could not find more beauty, more white sandy beaches, more lush vegetation, and clearer seas with coral reefs. The problem is the majority of the Caribbean people live in poverty. It is hard to understand why that is so. As I pointed out in Chapter 2, there may have been early civilizations that functioned for the benefit of the people but they were often enslaved or conquered by the early colonialists and pirates. Today only two island communities come to mind that have a high standard of living, the Caymans and Bermuda. Bermuda is actually located in the Atlantic. Let us discuss the possibilities for three western Caribbean nations.

Some Nations Competing in Caribbean

GUATEMALA	2000	2001	2002	2003	2004	2005	2006	2007	2008
GDP ($B)	$28	$29	$29	$30	$31	$32	$33	$35	$37
GROWTH (%)	3.6%	2.3%	2.2%	2.1%	2.7%	3.2%	5.3%	5.7%	4.4%
POPULATION (M)	11.1	11.3	11.5	11.7	11.9	12.2	12.5	12.7	13.0
PRODUCTIVITY ($)	$2,531	$2,544	$2,551	$2,557	$2,578	$2,608	$2,686	$2,780	$2,840

COSTA RICA	2000	2001	2002	2003	2004	2005	2006	2007	2008
GDP ($B)	$15	$15	$16	$17	$18	$19	$20	$22	$23
GROWTH (%)	1.8%	1.1%	2.9%	6.5%	4.2%	5.9%	8.8%	7.3%	4.3%
POPULATION (M)	3.7	3.8	3.8	3.9	4.0	4.0	4.1	4.1	4.2
PRODUCTIVITY ($)	$4,129	$4,104	$4,155	$4,356	$4,468	$4,662	$4,999	$5,289	$5,440

EL SALVADOR	2000	2001	2002	2003	2004	2005	2006	2007	2008
GDP ($B)	$15	$16	$16	$16	$16	$17	$18	$18	$19
GROWTH (%)	2.2%	1.7%	2.2%	1.8%	1.8%	2.8%	4.2%	4.7%	3.2%
POPULATION (M)	6.1	6.2	6.4	6.5	6.6	6.7	6.8	6.9	7.1
PRODUCTIVITY ($)	$2,488	$2,484	$2,493	$2,492	$2,493	$2,516	$2,576	$2,650	$2,690

Guatemala, Costa Rica, and El Salvador all suffer from leadership failures that have oppressed the people so badly they live below the poverty line. Costa Rica has the smallest population but operates at twice the GDP per person than either Guatemala or El Salvador. Many of these Caribbean countries compete in the agriculture and tourism segments of the world markets. Is it possible that Costa Rica has the better productivity because it entered the market segment that provides safe retirement communities in a tropical setting close to the American mainland?

When the Caymans offered financial services along with a tropical vacation community, their prosperity soared. Perhaps many of the Caribbean countries could benefit by participating in strategic planning outreach with America. These countries need to find high growth segments of the world markets that fit their capital, people, and physical resources and develop a strategic plan to set them on a path to prosperity.

I hope these few examples have shown you the benefits of *Compete and Empower* and the possibility that we can improve the prosperity of people in all nations. Let us now move on to a discussion of world peace. What is the current situation, and what are the possibilities?

CHAPTER SEVEN

A ROAD TO PEACE

"Peace has never come from dropping bombs. Real peace comes from enlightenment and educating people to behave more in a divine manner." **—Carlos Santana**

The world today is not a peaceful place. Governments of the two hundred-plus nations run the gamut from democracies to dictatorships with many variations in between. All of these nations have evolved from the Conquer and Oppress doctrine that has prevailed over the last 10,000 years.

CURRENT SITUATION

Even America, the most successful nation today, has deteriorated from its pure form of government of the people, by the people, and for the people established by our Founding Fathers to a democracy led by politicians and pundits who are oppressing the people. These leaders have set up a system to keep themselves in power so they can over-tax the people and fund pet social engineering projects that trap many citizens into a life of poverty. Instead of minimizing government and encouraging the individualism that made America great, they encourage people to depend on the government for their daily support.

Because the nations of the world have evolved by violent means and have rationalized their philosophy of government as best for the people, the elite leadership oppress the people while at the same time spinning their pure, fair, altruistic, and democratic intentions. At the beginning of the twenty-first century, when most individuals profess a propensity for peace, in many cases the inherent nature of our governments is to resolve conflicts through war. In the last century alone, there have been over seventy wars or conflicts, with the number of people killed ranging from thousands to millions.

The road to peace will not be easy because of the entrenched positions of the sovereign nations that make up the world today. There are three scenarios that provide a possible path to peace. They are: the current scenario where each nation administers its own justice and expects the UN nations to help resolve disputes when they get out of hand, the European scenario where each sovereign nation would subjugate its sovereignty to the UN and a world court in Europe, and the start again scenario that I believe has the best chance for success.

A ROAD TO PEACE HAS THREE SCENARIOS

1. **The Current Scenario …** A World Independent of
    the UN (WIUN)… This scenario describes the current
    circumstances. There are about two hundred sovereign
    nations, of which several are large and powerful. Each
    nation operates under its own system of laws. Many
    have powerful militaries. Most of the nations look to
    the United Nations (UN) to resolve disputes. Because
    the UN constitution is not helpful and its process
    is often blocked by veto, this institution has been
    ineffectual in many conflicts including ethnic cleansing.
    Also the UN has become a corrupt organization.
    Powerful nations will not subject their own sovereignty
    to a world order run by the UN.

2. **The European Scenario …** A world in Deference to
    the United Nations (DUN)… This is the preferred
    western European approach. Most of these nations
    have a military for defense but are unlikely to take on a
    leadership role in conflict resolution. Some of the time
    they will commit a small force to join a collaboration
    of the willing. America usually submits resolutions to
    the UN but reserves the right to go at it alone in its
    own self-interest. This scenario has proven unworkable
    as a serious possibility because of the UN's constitution,
    conflict resolution process, and inbred corruption.

3. **The Start Again Scenario …** A World of Empowered
    Nations (WEN)… This scenario requires that America
    leave the UN or minimize its involvement. America
    would then welcome its friends and allies to join WEN,
    encourage them to support *Compete and Empower,* and
    reject Conquer and Oppress. The nations forming this
    initial union would develop a WEN Constitution that

would enable peace to spread around the world. This scenario is the best with the most potential for a new world order.

EMBRACE *COMPETE AND EMPOWER* AND REJECT CONQUER AND OPPRESS

Although the path to a peaceful world seems impossible to navigate, I believe the doctrine of *Compete and Empower* can help us overcome such daunting challenges.

Challenging individuals to grow and prosper becomes the bedrock of better nations and a better world. Commercial enterprise provides the means to grow the wealth of a nation through individuals acting independently or organizing into businesses. Cooperating commercially on a global basis will spread peace and reject war. The wealth of a nation is the sum of its individuals, not the size and budget of its government. Although we can't expect all nations to function exactly the same because of their different history, culture, traditions, and evolution, it would help world prosperity if they adopted a free and open society similar in principle to the American Constitution.

Unfortunately there will probably always be fringe groups or nations that believe their interests are best served by terrorizing or conquering their citizens and threatening other countries. These rogue nations will keep their people in poverty and they will not meet the entry requirements of the new World of Empowered Nations (WEN).

Consequently, as we divine a peaceful path, it will most likely include a powerful force by each nation and an allied force amongst friends of WEN.

CAN AMERICA BE A ROLE MODEL?

Before we conclude that America can and should be a role model let us re-discover the vision of our Founding Fathers, ask if we're doing what they intended, and consider what needs to change so America can lead the world in the twenty-first century. America has the potential to be a role model but will need to make serious changes before this becomes a reality.

The Founding Fathers believed that the success of the nation came from the strength and character of the citizens and from successful businesses developed through hard work, productivity, and excellent products and services. It was expected that free market capitalism and trade would provide the best path to prosperity for these business enterprises. They also believed that the funding and management of appropriate local government services was the responsibility of citizen sponsorship of these services by local community, county, town, city, and state. Individuals or families that fell on hard times would be supported by friendship, local communities, and charities.

THE IDEA OF LIMITED FEDERAL GOVERNMENT

The Constitution calls for limited federal government with checks and balances to ensure that the people choose the level of funding and services and that the government leaders do not control the people. In their wisdom the Founding Fathers called for three major components of government, and a fourth component, the people organized in local communities, towns, cities, and states:

Article I. The legislative branch writes bills that become law based on the will of the people. It provides appropriate oversight and regulation as needed to ensure the integrity of law and order and is made up of the House of Representatives and the Senate.

Article II. The executive branch manages all funded functions of the government and is comprised of the president and the president's staff.

Article III. The judicial branch oversees all cases brought before the judiciary and ensures that the rule of law is followed. The courts involved are the Supreme Court and lower courts.

Article IV. The states ensure that all services determined by the will of the people in the state are administered within the state.

With our founders' interest in minimal federal government, it is reasonable to assume that they expected the president and members of Congress to be citizens, not career politicians. Although the president is limited to two four-year terms, it would be better for the democracy if the two terms became one eight-year term, thereby eliminating the need for reelection distractions. Senators and representatives should also be limited to one eight-year term. twenty-five percent of the total Congress should come up for election every two years to provide continuity and limit one-party power.

If we returned to the vision of our founders we would be more successful and be a better role model for the rest of the world: term limits for politicians, a nonunion government workforce, and no special retirement programs for all government employees and a more powerful military that can keep us safe. An America that lives the American dream and spreads *Compete and Empower* as its doctrine would be a great role model.

HOW DO WE DEFINE PEACE?

According to the Merriam-Webster dictionary, "peace" is a complex term with several levels of meaning:

A state of tranquility or quiet with freedom from civil disturbance. A state of security, order within a community.

An absence of war. A state or period of mutual concord between governments.

An article titled "The Nature of Peace and its Implications for Peace Education" by Leo R. Sandy and Ray Perkins Jr. lays out the complex nature of peace and can provide a more substantive tutorial on the subject.

CONCEPTS THAT CAN LEAD TO WORLD PEACE

I'll focus on the absence of war definition to develop an understanding of world peace and how *Compete and Empower* could improve upon the struggle of the last century. Mahatma Gandhi suggested that peace requires not only the absence of violence but also the presence of justice. Johan Galtung described this peace as "Peace with Justice" or positive peace. If nations compete commercially and are in a stable market as described by the *Compete and Empower* doctrine, then it is more likely that the competing nations will resolve their differences peacefully.

Along the way, individuals and a few governments have suggested initiatives or policies that could lead to world peace. Unfortunately, based on the results of the last century with over seventy conflicts and millions dead, our world of nations has been unable to embrace these suggestions and build a workable consensus that will sustain itself long term.

Peaceful periods were short lived. The longest period of relative peace in modern history was between the Napoleonic War of 1815 to the First World War of 1914. During this one-hundred year time frame, a majority of nations believed in free market capitalism.

Some of the solutions for peace that have been tried are summarized below:

- **Political …** Guide friends and allies by demonstrating through successful democracy that conflicts can be resolved without war.

- **Democratic …** Garner support for conflict resolution without war by showing persuasive empirical evidence that democracies never or rarely wage war with each other.

- **Capitalism …** Ayn Rand suggested that when a consensus of nations believed in capitalism, war was virtually eliminated as a method of conflict resolution.

- **Cobdenism …** Richard Cobden, an English statesman, suggested that free trade (laissez-faire) between countries would minimize the likelihood that they would use war to resolve conflicts.

- **Mutual Assured Destruction (MAD) …** MAD is a military strategy that makes war between nations pointless because both countries would be destroyed.

- **Isolationism …** Proponents of this solution suggest that nations that focus on their own domestic affairs tend not to impose their will on other nations, thereby causing major conflicts that could result in war.

- **Religious …** Most religious faiths preach a doctrine of peace based on man's love and respect for each other. This is a more passive solution and often results in war when an evil state decides it can take advantage of a weak neighbor.

SUGGESTIONS FOR THE ROAD AHEAD

We are at a fork in the road. Do we take the same road that has been well traveled for the last century? This path to peace and prosperity, WIUN has not served us well but appears to offer a pragmatic solution. Spreading *Compete and Empower* at the same time would improve the prosperity of the citizens of those nations that embrace it, but there would always be the concern that a more powerful nation could revert back to old habits of Conquer and Oppress.

Is there any reason to believe that WEN has a real possibility of working? Yes, there is! America has clearly demonstrated that entrepreneurial individuals supported by a constitution of limited government, framed by free market capitalism can build wealth and prosperity for all within a free and charitable society.

What observations can we make about the WEN solution? With the world at war against terrorism and no consensus among nations that the American version of democracy works or fits their culture, it is not surprising that there is widespread mistrust amongst nations.

The European Union has been trying for years to make its own union work, yet there are countries like the UK that are still not assimilated. It is easy to understand why Britain may prefer to stand alone. After all, they stood alone for two years,

1939 to 1941, at the beginning of World War II before the bombing of Pearl Harbor convinced the American Congress it was an American fight, too.

The League of Nations, founded in 1919, did not appear to work and was replaced by the United Nations (UN) in 1946. Although some UN activities have contributed to a better world, its lack of action against atrocities and its corruption in the Iraq Oil for Food Program render it an ineffective organization.

Some say the WEN approach will never work because there are too many countries, like America, who would never yield their sovereignty to a world government. The main problem in most attempts to unify some or all of disparate nations under a federated government body has been the ill-conceived constitution of these unions. For example in the UN the General Assembly each nation has one vote, independent of its size and contribution. In the Security Council, any member can veto any initiative. Is it any wonder that the UN can't act efficiently enough to stop ethnic cleansing or other atrocities?

The WEN road could lead to a utopia of world peace. There is a precedence set by the Constitution of the United States. In 1776, America declared itself independent of Britain. By September 17th, 1787, the Constitution had been signed by the delegates of eight states. By 2007, 220 years later, that system is still in place, and the United States has become the finest democracy the world has known.

The United States democracy survived many challenges throughout this period, including the Civil War over secession of the south and slavery, the civil rights movement over minority rights, and growth of the United States from eight to fifty states. All this was accomplished while the economy grew to over $14 trillion, three times greater than its nearest competitor. This growth occurred because most of the states were in one land mass and the country assimilated immigrants into a common culture with a common language. Perhaps the European Union may someday provide another constitutional precedence for the WEN to become a pragmatic reality.

Let us now consider the WIUN road and its strengths and weaknesses. First and foremost it fits the current circumstances. On the surface, there appears to be a modicum of stability and security. The two battles against terrorism in Iraq and Afghanistan appear to be manageable. Iraq continues toward a fragile but reasonable new democracy of sorts, providing Iran can be kept in check. Afghanistan requires reinforcements and a revised strategy in conjunction with the evolving concerns over Pakistan.

America can become more powerful, productive, and diplomatic if it embraces and acts on the principles of *Compete and Empower*. It is interesting to note that several of the solutions suggested earlier in this chapter are incorporated in the *Compete and Empower* doctrine. Although the WIUN idea of one powerful nation becoming the peacekeeper is not as palatable as the WEN solution, it is closer at hand and is more pragmatic.

(WEN) MAY BE A BETTER SOLUTION

Perhaps these two roads, WEN and WIUN, can be brought together into a four-lane highway in the future once the nations of the world have wandered alone in the wilderness for a while. Here are some suggestions that may be considered controversial but contain elements that people of good will can agree upon.

World leaders should get off the gravy-train high of Conquer and Oppress and embrace the doctrine of *Compete and Empower*.

This will develop a world that grows wealth and prosperity for all. Quit the failed ideas of nanny states where the all-powerful elite take care of the needs of the people. Encourage individualism and self-reliance at every opportunity. Show by example that each individual should learn, grow, and change every day in order to lead a fulfilling and prosperous life.

America could contribute the following:

- America will grow more prosperous and powerful by embracing the doctrine of *Compete and Empower,* thereby creating a future where we retain or exceed our world market share of GDP. We can show our friends and allies how to thrive as a great democracy and encourage them to follow suit in a way that is consistent with their culture and history.

- America will support diplomacy as a first step in conflict resolution around the world and will cooperate with any nation or group of nations on commercial enterprise and other endeavors if invited to do so.

- America will withdraw from the UN and stop funding it.

- America will form a new WEN with a new constitution that has a higher likelihood than the UN of working. The new WEN would encourage other countries to meet the entry criteria and participate in the benefits. Over time a growing majority of the world's nations could create a peaceful world under a new WEN framework.

- Until this utopia is reached, America will notify the world that it will continue to support all the treaties and conventions it currently supports, provided those treaties and conventions are in America's best interests. Furthermore the world will be notified that America reserves the right to act independently against atrocities affecting peace if it is in America's best interests.

Although highly controversial, the above five suggestions continue the status quo with action-oriented improvements. At the same time, they leave open the possibility that today's world could evolve into a world of prosperous growth for all individuals in a peaceful environment.

How can we reach this point? By following the strategic plan presented in the next chapter.

CHAPTER**EIGHT**

AN AMERICAN STRATEGIC PLAN

*Can a plan empower the country and perhaps
the world we live in?*

Developing a strategic plan for a single market business, a conglomerate business, or a nation is a process that involves the key contributors to the overall enterprise. A thoughtful book on this subject called *Building the Strategic Plan* by Stephanie K. Marrus is a how-to-do-it guide that will give you great tools and insight for preparing a plan and understanding the process. The process can take a few days to several months, involves a commitment by the top leaders to take it seriously, and can require substantial analysis to make sure the data is sound. The steps are: clarifying the mission, analyzing the current situation regarding the market and competition, setting goals and objectives, developing strategies and tactics and preparing measurable parameters for quarterly measurement and control.

I prefer to develop a strategic framework prior to the full plan preparation that includes all the subjects but requires the contributors to prepare the information collaboratively using their current knowledge and judgment. After completion, any items that need further in-depth analysis can be assigned to staff. A final, more detailed plan can then be prepared. I also prefer to separate the mission into a vision statement and a mission description. The table on the opposite page compares the strategic plan for a single business with a plan for a conglomerate or nation.

My purpose in writing this book has been to provide you with a strategic plan framework from my experience. Over the last forty years, I have met American citizens from all walks of life. We have discussed, collaborated, and reached conclusions on the "American Dream." In preparing this plan, I have followed the process outlined in the beginning of this chapter. The key contributors involved in the process are the American citizens I have collaborated with over the years. I intend to cover the subjects in the table noted with a check mark.

Once we embrace a strategic plan, we can use our initial short-term operating plan as a call to action for the "Citizen's Contract with America" outlined in Chapter 9.

I hope this sparks the spirit within you, especially those of you who still believe in the traditional America that I experienced in 1960. We can also encourage many progressives to think again about what has made America great and join our team.

Strategic Framework Comparison

Single Market Business Strategy	Multiple Market Nation Strategy
Vision	Vision ✔
Mission	Mission ✔
Current Situation	Current Situation ✔
Market	Market ✔
• Total Available (TAM)	• World GDP ✔
• Served Available (SAM)	• Served GDP ✔
• Growth	• Growth ✔
• Market Share	• GDP Share ✔
• Customer	• Core Business Clients
• External Trends	• External Trends
• Technology Trends	• Technology Trends
Competition	Core Competitors ✔
• Product	• Core Business Products
• Internal Assessment	• Internal Assessment
Goals	Goals ✔
• Sales	• GDP ✔
• Growth	• Growth ✔
• Profit	• Government Spend ✔
• People	• People ✔
• Productivity	• Productivity ✔
Strategy and Tactics	Strategy and Tactics ✔
Business Model	Business Model ✔
Pro-Forma Financials	Pro-Forma Financials
Valuation	Valuation
Next Step	Next Step ✔
Operating Plan	Operating Plan

✔ Checkmarks identify those elements that are described in this chapter

VISION

*An American vision honoring
our Founding Fathers ...*

America becomes a guiding light in a planet where peace is embraced by all the people because of America's success. Our Founding Fathers gift was a constitution that makes possible justice for all and holds as self-evident that all men are created equal, that they are endowed by their Creator with certain unalienable rights, and that among these are life, liberty, and the pursuit of happiness.

★ ★ ★ ★

MISSION

A mission that leads to our vision
for the future ...

America intends to transform its current leadership into a nation, indivisible, that demonstrates its principles for success by maintaining or exceeding its world market share through the twenty-first century and beyond. By following a new *Compete and Empower* doctrine, it will show by example how the world market can be divided into segments where all nations can compete and prosper.

As a generous nation, America will share its experience with those nations considered friends or allies and who show an interest in participating with the United States. Those nations that embrace the new doctrine, and America as a friend, will realize improved productivity and prosperity for their people. As trust grows and results are achieved a World of Empowered Nations (WEN) will emerge.

America is committed to bring to justice those individuals or nations that commit atrocities against their own citizens or those of other nations.

★ ★ ★ ★

CURRENT SITUATION

The current situation …

In 2009 America and the world is facing a financial crisis of serious proportions. A progressive, liberal solution is being proposed by the current administration, Congress, and Senate that changes a dynamic, self-reliant nation into a slow-growth, socialist state like Western Europe.

THE STATUS OF WORLD MARKET SHARE

In the early 1800s, America had a smaller share of world GDP than China, many Western European nations, India, and Japan. Today America has three times the market share of China and Japan and significantly more than all the Western European nations and India. Out of a world GDP of $52 trillion the United States has over $14 trillion.

At this time, world GDP appears to be growing, on average, at 5 percent. During this period of financial crisis, it's possible that we could see one or two years of negative growth, but over a fifty-year period in the future with emerging nations growing rapidly the average should be at least 5 percent. America has a population of about 300 million with a high productivity over $45,000 per citizen whereas China has a population of 1,400 million with a low productivity about $2,000. Current expert opinion suggests that America's GDP growth in the future will be less than world GDP growth and therefore America's market share will decline.

China's market share will overtake America's in 2035 because China is still expected to grow GDP at rates over 7 percent, significantly more than world GDP. Note that American market share also declined in the 1980s when expert opinion expected Japan to overcome America.

America recovered to 28 percent because Japan floundered, propping up its banks in the 1990–1991 recession. If America had made GDP growth its highest priority, then America would have maintained or exceeded its position as Japan grew.

Historical Market Share Current Situation

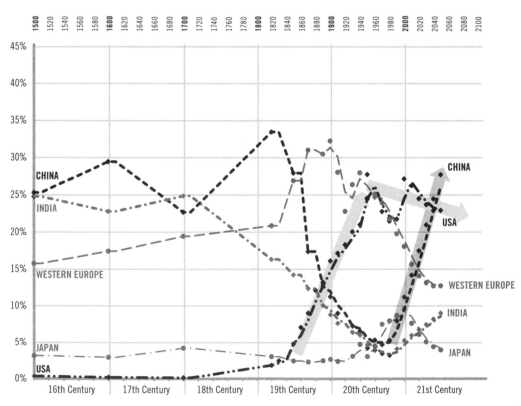

AMERICAN CURRENT ATTRIBUTES

Even in a chaotic twentieth century of dictatorships, communism, socialism, wars, and appeasement around the world, America has risen to become the leader. Why? Because of America's attributes:

- A constitution that supports freedom, individualism, and free market capitalism.

- Creative people with character, courage, and a spirit of hard work, integrity, tradition, and entrepreneurship.

- A business philosophy of free market capitalism.

- A powerful military well trained in the latest technology and patriotic in their duty to defend our freedom.

- Businesses that innovate, develop, produce, and use the latest technology.

- Many business leaders who motivate their organizations to grow and succeed for all stakeholders and communicate company strategy and plans down through the company.

- The best medical technology.

- Skilled local professionals in police, fire, justice, community planning, and other public services that protect the people.

- Charitable people and organizations that support people in need when catastrophic emergencies occur.

AMERICA IS LOSING GROUND IN THE CURRENT CRISIS

America held its share of world GDP from 2005 to 2007. Using data from the Bureau of Economic Analysis (BEA) and some estimates we find the following:

Word GDP with U.S. Market Share

YEAR	2005	2006	2007	2008	2009 Forecast
World GDP $	$45.3	$47.6	$50.0	$52.5	$52.5
Growth	5.0%	5.0%	5.0%	5.0%	0.0%
U.S. GDP $	$12.7	$13.4	$14.0	$14.2	$13.5
Growth	6.3%	5.3%	4.9%	1.2%	<-5.0%>
U.S. Market Share	28%	28.1%	28.1%	27.1%	25.7%

$ in trillions

A slow down in the economy started in 2008 and sent America into a tailspin when Lehman Brothers failed and the Treasury secretary and the Congress panicked and requested emergency funds, called TARP, of $700 billion to solve the sub-prime mortgage challenge. In September 2008, job losses accelerated to over 600,000 per month and peaked in December at over 700,000. Starting in February 2009, the economy appeared to be improving with job losses dropping to 322,000 per month. We are not out of the woods yet because in June job losses jumped to 467,000 and the unemployment rate was 9.5 percent.

Because China and a few other nations are growing faster than world GDP, America's market share has stated to slip. It dropped to 27.1 percent in 2008 and is estimated to drop to 25.7 percent in 2009. With America in such a large leadership position economically, the rest of the world is affected when

America slows down. Those nations that have supported a Conquer and Oppress philosophy and gone down the road to socialism are the hardest hit from our contraction because they are unable to respond quickly.

China is clearly an anomaly. It has a central communist government with state-owned businesses. Yet twenty-five-years ago, it set GDP growth as its highest priority, started liquidating their state-owned businesses, and freed up its people to become entrepreneurs and grow a free market.

THE CHALLENGES FACING AMERICA TODAY

As I said in the beginning, my intention is to be clear about the facts, historically, and currently, and let the data drive the conclusions. At the present time, I am convinced that the barriers to resolving the challenges we face are our leaders. The 535 politicians who have put themselves in charge, both Democrat and Republican along with their staff, should be held accountable for America's recent results. Because they do as they please and do not serve the public, they must be retired by term limits. We must find bold, fresh young representatives who will support the people and their businesses.

The challenges we face are even more daunting because of the results of the last election. The people voted the most liberal progressive politicians into power since Roosevelt. What's worse is that they put a young charismatic, college professor and community leader with no business experience and no understanding of the way the world works into the presidency. This naive person is grabbing power left and right and pushing through a socialist agenda, which will crush the American dream.

He told us on the campaign trail that this is what he was going to do, but only a few were listening. The majority was caught up in the glamour and charisma. The media are the real culprits in this pied piper charade. They have not honored their constitutional duty to be critical of every move. They took sides and became the mouthpiece for the candidate. Now that he is in office, they will not dig deep and verify the truth because they are culpable.

A WATERSHED MOMENT FOR AMERICA

In summary the current situation is a watershed for the American people. On the one hand we are still the most successful democracy the world has ever known and we are the strongest economically. We have a patriotic, competent military. We have been free, but are losing our freedoms daily, and we are extremely charitable. On the other hand we face very serious challenges and are going in the wrong direction. We must stop the current chaos created by politicians trying to get their socialist program through at any cost to the nation. My intention is to show you how a *Compete and Empower* strategic plan, followed by a call to action, can overcome the challenges.

MARKET
The current market situation ...

In 2009 many expert economists believe world GDP growth will increase 0 percent in 2009 over 2008 and -1.3 percent in 2010. The GDP $ value per year is shown at the end of each decade. This is based on the assumption that world GDP will grow at the same average rate as the last fifty years.

World GDP Growth Estimate

Year Start	2009	2011	2021	2031	2041
Year End	2010	2020	2030	2040	2050
World GDP	**$51.8**	**$84.4**	**$137.6**	**$224.1**	**$365.0**
Growth/Year	<-1.3%>	5.0%	5.0%	5.0%	5.0%

$ In trillions

In my opinion, this could be significantly higher than 5 percent if many nations embrace *Compete and Empower* and enter the free market. The world GDP growth rate could be less if America gets bogged down in rejecting socialism and most countries reject natural competition as a path to prosperity. America's current leadership, press, and economic experts have already declared defeat against China.

Read the editorials in our newspapers, and listen to the pundits and politicians on TV prime time and on the news channels, and you will soon get the message. The twenty-first century will be the China century. China will overtake us in thirty years. Because of this defeatist attitude, our politicians do not deserve to lead this great country of ours. They must be replaced with politicians, journalists, and economists who believe in America and are not part of the "blame America" first crowd that wants to continually rewrite history.

Population Growth Current Situation

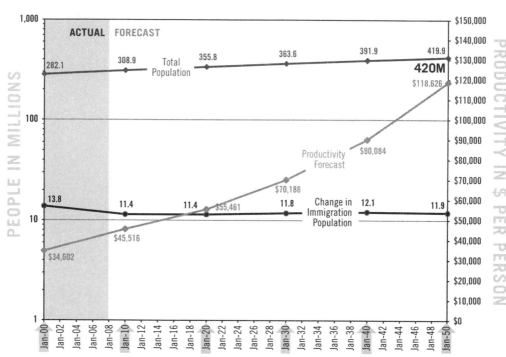

IMMIGRATION POLICY IS IMPORTANT

The chart above shows that United States population only grows to 420 million by 2050, based on current immigration policy.

Even this slow growth approach to our future requires an increase in immigration of about 1 million people per year. Under the current immigration policy, we have accumulated 15 to 20 million illegal immigrants in the last twenty years since the amnesty under Reagan. We must change the policy to provide green cards for all immigrants, set the level per year to fit the strategic plan, and make the highest priority based on job skill requirements as determined by American businesses.

Based on so-called expert estimates of population, reasonable productivity growth, and annual growth rates below 5 percent, our leaders only expect America to grow to $49.8 trillion by 2050. Alan Greenspan in his recent book, *The Age of Turbulence,* also supported this slow growth America theme. He estimates America's GDP at about $25 trillion by 2030 and expects China to overtake us by 2035. Using a growth rate for China consistent with the last twenty years, expert opinion suggests China will reach $94.3 billion by 2050. It doesn't have to play out this way. With a strategic plan, we can maintain or exceed our current market share for the rest of this century.

GDP Growth Current Situation

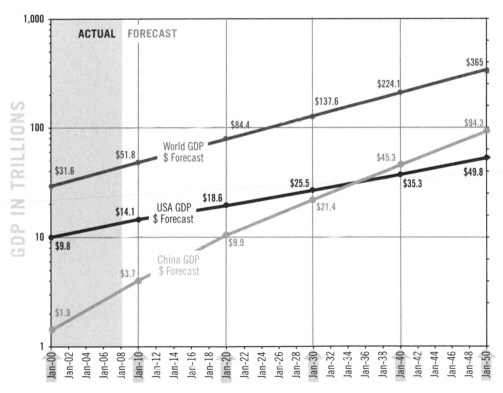

Market Share Current Situation

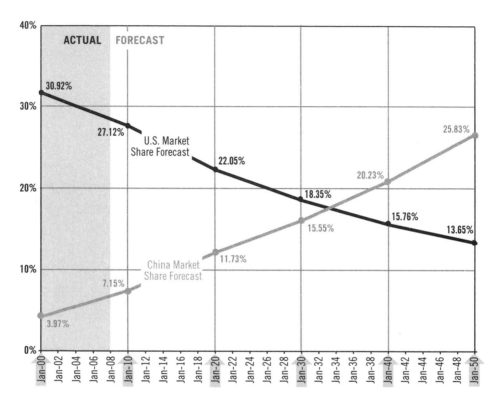

MARKET SHARE PRINCIPLES

Finally the current market conditions, the current state of our government, and the belief of our leaders portray a bleak future for the twenty-first century. This situation is best displayed by the market shares of America and China based on the prior data.

According to the principles of natural and strategic competition, the world will face an unstable market for twenty years, from 2025 to 2045. Currently the world market is dominated by three large players: America, Japan, and China. America is clearly the leader at three times the size of Japan and China. However Japan is asleep at the wheel and China has serious strategic intent to be the largest nation in the world. Today Japan and China are similar in size with Japan stagnant and China growing fast. It is only a matter of time until China becomes a strong #2 and Japan #3.

If China is determined to become #1 and America has already accepted defeat, then the market will be unstable from 2025 to 2045, changing allegiances and disrupting smaller nations. The smaller nations, if they adopt the *Compete and Empower* philosophy, can find a safe haven in a smaller market segment where they can compete effectively. A problem could occur if the two top competitors enter into a dog fight and act irrationally, taking up arms to resolve disputes.

Because it is very difficult and expensive to change market share, America must retain its rightful place as world leader and embrace a strategic plan that ensures such a result at the same time that China continues its course to lift its people out of poverty. The end result will be a stable market with three or four major players. They will be satisfied with their positions because their goals are met and they cooperate commercially with each other.

CORE COMPETITORS
Competition at the top of the world is challenging ...

According to data from the BEA and the U.S. Department of Agriculture (USDA) in 2008, the fifteen largest nations competing for the top three or four spots were as follows:

GDP, Marketshare, Population, and Productivity— Top 15 Nations

Rank	Nation	2007 GDP	MARKET SHARE	MILLIONS POPULATION	$ PRODUCTIVITY
	WORLD TOTAL	$49.5	100.0%	6,500	$7,000
Rank	Nation				$ In trillions
1	UNITED STATES	$13.9	28.1%	304	$45,900
2	JAPAN	$4.5	9.1%	127	$35,242
3	CHINA	$3.1	6.3%	1,330	$2,350
4	GERMANY	$3.0	6.1%	82	$36,387
5	UK	$2.4	4.8%	61	$39,207
6	FRANCE	$2.3	4.6%	64	$35,427
7	ITALY	$1.8	3.6%	58	$30,988
8	CANADA	$1.3	2.6%	33	38,596
9	SPAIN	$1.3	2.6%	40	$30,547
10	BRAZIL	$1.1	2.2%	196	$5,736
11	INDIA	$1.0	2.0%	1,148	$849
12	S. KOREA	$1.0	2.0%	48	$20,102
13	RUSSIA	$1.0	2.0%	141	$6,749
14	MEXICO	$0.8	1.6%	110	$7,687
15	AUSTRALIA	$0.8	1.6%	21	$30,758

Data from different sources may differ somewhat, but in strategic planning we are looking to identify positions or trends where the absolute value is not as important as the direction.

MARKET SEGMENTS

Following the principles of natural competition, and assuming that about two hundred nations are competing, you would expect to find thousands of segments of three or four main competitors. Each segment will end up with different characteristics. Each segment may well have some minor players, either leaving to enter another segment, or entering to shake things up and become a market leader. Each nation will have a portfolio of businesses that make up the nation's total GDP. If each nation develops a sound strategy within its resource limits and invests any excess cash quickly and wisely, then the wealth of each nation will grow. Those nations that continue to oppress their people confiscate the cash from the productive businesses and waste it on saber rattling or social engineering will keep their people in poverty. Our purpose in this segment is to focus on the competitors that have a realistic opportunity to be in the top of the world segment for size and growth.

THE TOP OF THE WORLD SEGMENT

United States ... Clearly the leader of the world from an economic performance perspective, the nation has serious challenges ahead because of the leadership. The current administration and political power players are bent on taking the country into more Conquer and Oppress policies that will smother the freedom and dynamism that has made the nation great. It remains to be seen whether the Constitution and the character of the people will be enough strength to hold America's world leadership.

Japan ... Currently Japan has the second largest GDP.
Opinion says its bureaucracy will not allow it to make the
changes necessary to stay in a strong #2 position. Japan
demonstrated how powerful it can be in the 1980s when it
grew rapidly, developed terrific technology, demonstrated
the results of TQM, and increased market share. Japan's
challenges are to respond quickly and strongly to systemic
problems in the financial area and to solve its aging
demographics issues with an aggressive immigration
policy. Current opinion suggests that it will not respond
appropriately to the challenges of the twenty-first century
and will lose out to the rougher and tumble competitors
in this segment. Through *Compete and Empower,* it could
define a new segment and be its leader.

China ... It is very difficult to know the "behind the scenes"
thinking of the Chinese government. It is a single-party
communist dictatorship and are therefore unpredictable.
All we can do is follow its actions and the results. I also
found it helpful to visit several cities in China and talk to
the people. China is clearly the most important challenger
for leadership of the top of the world segment. Although
the regime follows the Conquer and Oppress doctrine, the
country has an interesting strategy designed to raise the
bulk of its population out of poverty. Its strategy, starting
twenty-five years ago, was to set GDP growth high and set
the people free to become entrepreneurs and to participate
in a free market capital system. The performance is superb
and the people, with the government's support, are getting
the job done. In a way it is *compartmentalized freedom.* The
young people support their government and have set lower
priorities on all the politically correct issues that take up
the time of the American leadership.

Western Europe And Remnants Of The British Empire ...
Germany, Britain, France, Italy, Canada, Spain, and
Australia all have "wannabe" aspirations to compete in the
top of the world segment. Current opinion does not take
them seriously. They play at power politics but behave like
lost souls from periods past, at a time when they were truly
powerful and dominated the world for centuries. In some
cases, they have a large GDP and are reasonably productive.
So where have they gone wrong? Their governments,
exercising power through Conquer and Oppress policy,
allowed the socialist dogma to creep into their institutions
in the last century. They are comfortable enough to exist
but not proud enough to challenge the status quo of slow
growth and mediocre results. Their comfort with the
current circumstances may lead to their further decline.
Their policies of tolerance and appeasement are allowing
infiltration by Muslim extremists under the politically
correct idea of multiculturalism. To play a role in the top of
the world segment this century, they will need completely
new leadership to shake things up. The last prime minister
of Australia was this type of person. Will his policies have
staying power? Time will tell. Their other opportunity is to
refocus and play in differently defined segments where they
can be successful with revitalized strategies.

Brazil ... Current experts hold Brazil in high esteem as a
potential challenger because of its high GDP growth over
at least a decade. This country is often highlighted as a
good place to invest and is called one of the BRIC high,
growth nations. BRIC stands for Brazil, Russia, India,
and China. Brazil is starting at a much lower level than
China and will have a difficult time catching up even with
realistic high-growth rates. The leadership must lift its
people out of poverty from a $5,736 level. The country

owns large amounts of natural resources that can be a source of wealth by adding labor or by selling the resources for cash on the open market. Concern holding the country back is the political turmoil in neighboring nations and whether the leadership has the staying power to embrace *Compete and Empower*.

Russia ... Russia, like China, could be an interesting competitor. Many of its young people are smart, energized, and powerful competitors. The country has substantial natural resources that are being used to its advantage. It has potential for good selective great technology. Look at remnants from the Cold War. Unfortunately Russia is the poster boy for Conquer and Oppress. The world had high hopes for Russia to become a significant contributor to world prosperity, but today it appears to have returned to its old ways and supports a very corrupt system.

India ... India is another country that has great potential. Its population is almost as large as China with a need to lift the majority of its citizens out of poverty. Over the last decade, it has been growing its GDP rapidly and has introduced technology centers that support world markets. Its smart and well-educated citizens show what can be done with new enlightened policies. The country's institutions are bureaucratic and can hold the country back. India should carefully weigh its resources, consider how well it is doing in its markets, and redefine a new segment where it can more successfully compete.

GOALS

Goals that achieve the mission ...

In order to meet our aspirations for America, we must set goals that lead to a victorious completion of the mission. The goals will require us to change the status quo. We must rise above partisan politics and do what's best for the country. We will set challenging goals that we intend to meet or exceed.

AMERICA'S GDP GROWTH TO EQUAL OR EXCEED
THE WORLD RATE

This goal will ensure that the United States retains world leadership for the twenty-first century and the foreseeable future. It will support China's growth goals and stabilize the top of the world segment. The next chart shows the result of this goal from a historical perspective, and the future forecast shows improvement in market share.

Historical Market Share American Strategy

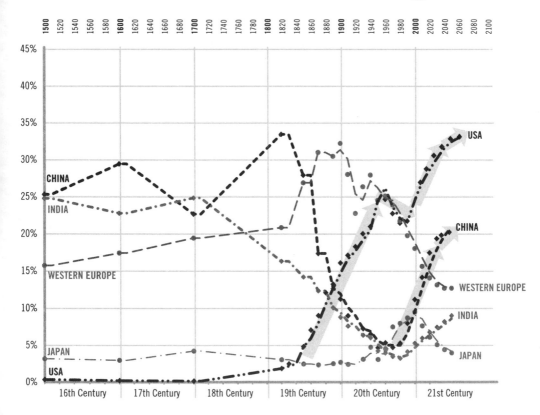

The GDP goal in $ through 2050 can be seen in the next chart where it is compared to world GDP and China. China is able to maintain its high growth until it settles into a stable position as number two.

GDP Growth American Strategy

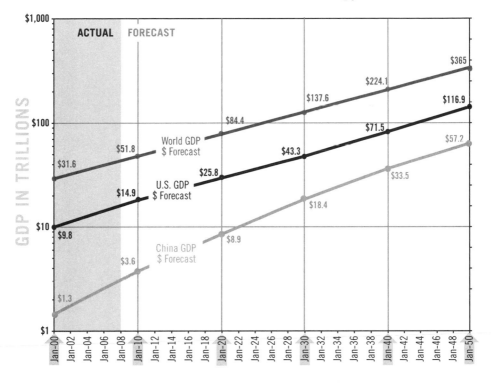

THE UNITED STATES'S MARKET SHARE
TO INCREASE TO 32 PERCENT BY 2050

This challenging goal will ensure a natural competition stable market.

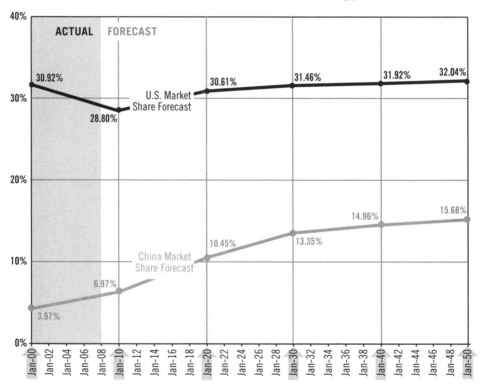

Market Share American Strategy

INCREASE PRODUCTIVITY OF THE PEOPLE
TO $140,000 BY 2050

Historically, productivity has been improving in the United States every year. For this goal, I used 3 percent per year improvement as a reasonable expectation. In order to meet the primary GDP, goal immigration must increase significantly

Population Growth American Strategy

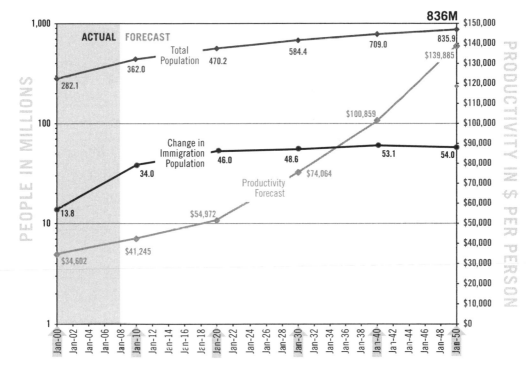

INCREASE POPULATION TO 836 MILLION BY 2050

The primary goal is to increase the GDP. In order to achieve the GDP goal proposed with a reasonable productivity of $140,000 per person, then we will need over 800 million people of a variety of skills to get the job done. If we improve productivity at a higher rate, we would not need as many people. In order to accomplish this goal and reach a GDP of over $100 trillion by 2050, we would need to increase legal immigration to about five million per year and assimilate them. This is five times the current rate.

TRANSFORM GOVERNMENT TO A
COMPETE AND EMPOWER DOCTRINE

Develop a Strategic Planning Outreach Team (SPOT) in the Commerce Department led by the Secretary of Commerce.

REDUCE FEDERAL GOVERNMENT SPENDING
TO 11 PERCENT OF GDP

Support a strong military and defense to a level of 5 percent of GDP. Hold federal spending on overhead and employment for government programs to 5 percent and reduce all welfare to a safety net level of 1 percent including Medicaid. Reduce the national debt to zero in 20 years.

CONVERT SOCIAL SECURITY AND MEDICARE TO INVESTMENT PROGRAMS

Stop putting people's payments into the general fund. If the citizens prefer a forced savings program by the government, then the funds should be invested for the citizen's account. The citizen would own the account. Both Social Security and Medicare become balance sheet items not mandatory spending.

CONVERT FOREIGN AID TO A VENTURE INVESTMENT PROGRAM

Invest in a nation's businesses. Do not send checks to a nation's government. Support businesses that have come from nations supporting *Compete and Empower* and are using the American Strategic Planning Outreach Team (SPOT).

SELL ALL FEDERALLY RUN BUSINESSES TO THE PRIVATE SECTOR

This goal includes the following businesses: banks, autos, schools, postal service, insurance, and charity.

REFORM LAWMAKING

Review all laws on the books today, and remove all that are not working, not useful, or are not acted on by law enforcement. Terminate union law, and give unions the option of going out of business or becoming trade associations. Reform torte law practice to eliminate waste and fraud.

★ ★ ★ ★

STRATEGY AND TACTICS

*Strategy is a broad direction to
achieve our goals ...*

I have selected the ten most important strategies that will dramatically move our country back to the founders' vision, principles, and Constitution. We will reject the people who have
usurped control from "we, the people" and will replace them
with public servants who will honor the oath of office and serve
the citizens with integrity. These ten strategies will be backed
up in Chapter 9 with a proposed new "Citizen's Contract with
America," our operating plan we'll use to ensure we succeed.

Ten Strategies To Transform America from Conquer and Oppress to *Compete and Empower*.

1. **Transform the Federal Government by:** replacing
    career politicians with citizen politicians, removing
    arcane rules that reduce results, eliminating
    unnecessary staffs and organizations, and placing all
    government employees including politicians on the
    same Social Security and Medicare programs as every
    other citizen.

2. **Support American Businesses so They Can Grow
    GDP Faster than World GDP and Increase Market
    Share by:** reallocating resources in the commerce
    department to fund a Strategic Planning Outreach

Team (SPOT), annually developing a plan in second quarter and sharing it with the public, improving prosperity, and making citizens aware of our goal to *Compete and Empower.*

3. **Change the Tax Law and Reduce Spending by:** enacting the "Fair Tax Proposal" into law, requiring zero-based budgeting with ROI requirements and monthly measurements of performance for spending projects, and eliminating all unnecessary staff and organizations.

4. **Eliminate all Unions by:** changing the labor laws so that unions are either required to go out of business or transform into trade associations.

5. **Increase Legal Immigration To Support our Plan for Skilled Employees by:** providing a barrier to illegal entry, enacting immigration laws that provide green cards to support the GDP growth plan, (prioritized on the basis of employment skills and American business needs), resolving the current illegal immigrant challenge by punishing the crime, and offering them an opportunity to compete with all comers for the jobs needed to meet our strategic plan.

6. **Provide a Superior Military and Security Team by:** fully funding (5 percent of GDP) all resources required to win wars and execute military missions as needed to support our twenty-first-century strategic plan, using the latest technology, and eliminating all barriers to acquiring intelligence that protects our people.

7. **Transform the State Department from Diplomatic "Do Little" to Managed Action and Results by:** approaching rogue nations from strength not weakness, expecting proposals that solve problems to be taken seriously or there will be consequences, changing policy to solutions that provide long-term peace with integrity not short-term stability without honor, promoting *Compete and Empower* to friends and allies, and requiring that all foreign aid be invested into businesses supported by SPOT instead of given to governments as bribes for better behavior.

8. **Resolve Social Security and Medicare Challenges by:** acknowledging that they are improperly funded Ponzi schemes set up and managed by politicians, transferring all assets and liabilities to investment funds owned by the citizens and managed by professionals, improving the return to the citizens, resolving any imbalances between investment into the funds and withdrawal from the funds, and moving these programs from mandatory spending accounts to balance sheet accounts.

9. **Improve the Performance of Government-Run Businesses by:** selling all businesses (banks, insurance, automobile, schools, and post office at a minimum) to private citizens via a series of public offerings managed by American investment bankers, and managing with professionals the defense, foreign aid venture funds, safety net venture funds, and safety net charitable welfare businesses.

10. **Manage Safety Net Business for Performance by:** hiring professional managers from the venture fund and charity fund industries, funding at 1 percent of GDP, requiring welfare recipients to present a plan for getting off welfare, and educating people with true hardships and disabilities how to obtain charitable support from family, friends, and neighborhood charities before coming to the government as a last resort.

BUSINESS MODEL

A prosperous business model ...

Understanding the business model is essential to predicting whether we will have a long-term business success. The chart on the following page shows the relationships between the elements of the nation's business. The engine of growth, wealth, and prosperity are the American people and their businesses. We have become the dominant market share nation because of the leadership by our businesses. To put this business model in perspective, compare it to a very large conglomerate with many businesses reporting in to a corporate staff and chief executive.

An American Business Model

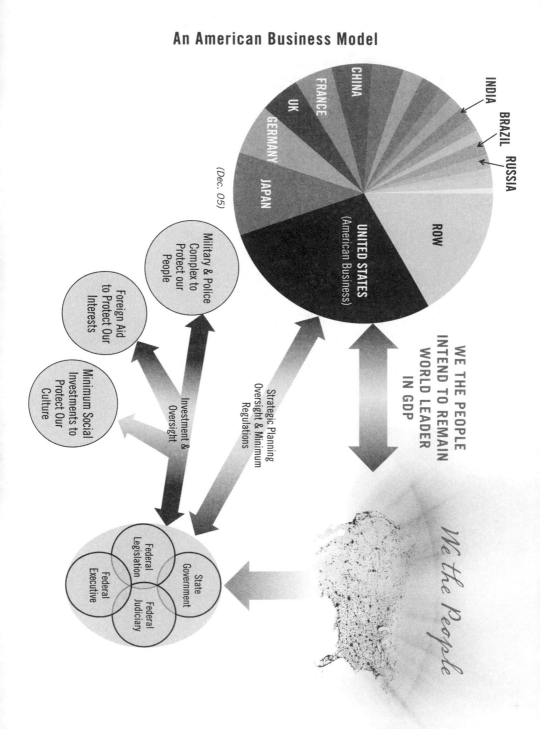

(Dec. 05)

INDIA
BRAZIL
RUSSIA

CHINA
FRANCE
UK
GERMANY
JAPAN

ROW

UNITED STATES
(American Business)

Military & Police
Complex to
Protect our
People

Foreign Aid
to Protect Our
Interests

Minimum Social
Investments to
Protect Our
Culture

Investment &
Oversight

Strategic Planning
Oversight & Minimum
Regulations

WE THE PEOPLE
INTEND TO REMAIN
WORLD LEADER
IN GDP

Federal
Legislation

Federal
Executive

State
Government

Federal
Judiciary

We the People

The government functions shown can be considered a headquarters corporate staff to ensure that the whole conglomerate functions profitably and protects the conglomerate from external barriers, bureaucracy, and threats. A conglomerate headquarters staff may have many other functions, including planning, oversight, and compliance to rules and regulations. The range of corporate headquarters' overhead in most cases is one to six percent of total sales.

In contrast, our federal government is wasteful, is considerably more bloated, and acts as a drag on the economy. If our government functioned at 11 percent instead of over 30 percent of GDP, think how profitable and dynamic our economy would be. Unfortunately as a result of one hundred years of manipulation and neglect, we now spend over $3.4 trillion (24 percent) out of a $14.2 trillion GDP on government. Our business model is good for any nation that wants to succeed, but government must be transformed to serve the people, not government employees and politicians.

People are better served when important policy decisions are made by the individuals and corporations responsible for success in the free market. The government should perform no more than a staff function does in business enterprises. People will receive a better, more honest deal from business people than from self-serving politicians and government bureaucrats. Of course there are often bad apples in the barrel that spoil the reputation of the whole barrel, and this is true for both business and government. The point is that although there are principled business people, politicians, and government bureaucrats, the government should not be in charge of the wealth and prosperity of the nation. It should be in a supporting role.

The brilliance of our Constitution is in the balance it provides by establishing government by the people. I believe that it was the founders' intent that the people hire and fire the president, vice president, and members of the House and Senate by voting them in or out of office. The founders expected the politicians to be term limited and if citizens, committed to public service, committed to serve as a politician, they would return to private practice after serving their term. Unfortunately we have seen the growth of career politicians who have found ways to gerry-mander the voting so that they stay in office to a ripe old age, when in most cases their capabilities are diminished and they are not capable of doing the job.

Another wonderful aspect of the Constitution is how it lets the majority rule but provides a means for minority voices to be heard. But because politicians have found ways to cobble together coalitions of minorities to carry them to winning campaigns, we end up with a form of minority rule over the majority's expectations. If we are to have a clear and unambig-uous first priority to grow the wealth and prosperity of the nation and retain our world leadership, we do not need a government that thinks it's in charge and has taken control from the people.

Politicians have hired a bloated bureaucracy to retain their power. In addition, politicians set up processes so that minority special interests fund specific politicians who then support programs to override the majority. The same challenges face state and local governments as well.

The business model can work well for the benefit of all the people if we require our government to follow the conglomerate version of this model and operate in a similar fashion to Warren Buffet's governance of Berkshire Hathaway.

THE NEXT STEP

What happens next ...?

We now have a strategic plan framework based on the judgment of the participants. The next step is to get feedback from you, the citizens, on the merit of the plan and on ideas for improvement. Please go to www.briansbusinessblog.com and post your contribution.

Finally we go to Chapter 9 to understand that we can act on this plan by enacting a new "Citizen's Contract with America."

CHAPTER NINE

SENSIBLE SOLUTIONS

*"In this present crisis, government is not the solution;
government is the problem."*
—Ronald Reagan, First Inaugural Address

America is ready to lead the world into a better future. Earlier
chapters of this book have explored the necessary elements of a
successful society:

Five elements of a successful society:

1. A constitution that calls for freedom of its people and
   puts them in charge of the government.

2. A strategic plan that capitalizes on natural competition
   and embraces *Compete and Empower*.

3. The character of the people and the culture they created.

4. Recognition that free market capitalism is the only path
   that creates wealth and prosperity for all its citizens.

5. Leaders of the people and the government should embrace honesty, integrity, and wisdom, and show courage and commonsense by stopping practices that don't work and supporting ideas that do.

AMERICAN EXCEPTIONALISM

Over the last one hundred years, America has been more successful than any other nation. Our GDP is three times larger than any other nation; we are eighth out of over two hundred nations in wealth/productivity per person; our military is strong and resourceful; our people have more freedoms than most and we are very charitable.

While the results from the first three elements above have been outstanding, our leaders have been lacking in many ways. Some citizens have said that it's good when we have a "do nothing" Congress because if they did act we'd be in a worse mess than we are now. Others have said our leaders and their rules are good because the pendulum swings from too much socialism to too much self-reliance and settles somewhere in the middle. Instead what we need is professional, smart, transparent, and honest leadership that follows the spirit of the Constitution and the Founding Fathers.

Once again let's recognize that we are the world leader and its okay to hold our heads high and stop the self-recrimination about mistakes we may or may not have made. The question is do we, the American people, have the courage to challenge the leadership of our country and the systems they've put in place, and to replace those currently in power?

The sensible solutions proposed in this chapter are more revolutionary than evolutionary. In order for the reader to consider the solutions seriously, it is helpful to describe the current situation as a context in which to judge them.

CURRENT SITUATION REGARDING AMERICAN LEADERSHIP

Our politicians are polarized between socialism and conservatism. Both political parties have gerrymandered the system so that they stay in power and vote for the agendas of special interests that fund their campaigns. As a result, the majority often loses out and then loses interest in the political process. As a result, it is difficult to get over fifty percent of the voting public to vote. We must replace all career politicians with citizen politicians who are committed to serve the people as public servants.

The rules of order, traditions, committees, and subcommittees set up by the House and Senate are so convoluted that they stop important work of the people from getting done. The politicians seem to have lost all sense of responsibility.

How big a staff do they need? How many investigations need to be run? How many committees are needed? Judging by the amount of time they are *not* on the job, and by the amount of time spent pontificating on committees, it's clear they do not care about the return on taxpayers' investment. Today a senator or representative, on a salary of $174,000, spends an average of $2.5 million on overhead and staff to help him do his job. Is it any wonder he can take so much time off? Then they grandstand about salaries and bonuses in private industry.

What company would hire an employee for a four-year contract and allow the employee to virtually take two years off with pay in order to prepare for another job? It happens in Congress, and the taxpayer foots the bill. It happened in the last election cycle for president. Why do we not question the integrity and morality of an individual who would even consider not fulfilling his contract without resigning? Such behavior is not becoming of an American president.

Although the Constitution puts the people in charge, politicians, and the executive branch believe they are in charge and act accordingly. They often behave as elitists and work to divide the country into two classes: the workers and the elite. On the other hand, American businesses embrace all employees in hundreds of different jobs with all levels of pay from entry-level to CEO. All the employees are part of a strategic team.

Instead of appreciating business performance, the politician talks of division, that the rich are getting richer and the workers are getting poorer. This classic case of lying with statistics is lapped up by the press without any probing questions. If a business doubles in size, the pay of an entry-level job only grows by the inflation rate (CPI). However the company has added thousands of jobs, many of them high-responsibility, high-paying jobs. With such success, the CEO is rewarded by increased compensation, the employees benefit with more high-paying jobs, and the country benefits because the growth improves the United States share of the world market.

Imagine the entry-level employee, Miss Malleable, who looks up the corporate ladder and sees job opportunities galore. All she need do is learn, grow, and change and she'll have a bright future with ever-increasing compensation. Or she could become a second-class citizen when a union employee presents

Miss Malleable with the union pitch: "If you join the union you'll get union wages." However she will take a cut in union pay and contribute a percentage of her wages to the union. The union will use her dues to fund politicians who promise a minimum wage increase. In addition the union will negotiate work rules to make her life on the job easier, as well as providing benefits for life. They will even present her to society as a victim, a downtrodden worker.

The original American dream was to take the path to opportunity and self-reliance. Unfortunately, today too many malleable youngsters are swayed by the political and union elites to select victimization and sign up to vote for the nanny state and dependence on a handout.

The national press was given, in the Constitution, an awesome responsibility to be objective. This responsibility is called "Freedom of the Press." Perhaps the press was just as biased one hundred years ago but with today's twenty four-hour television it's easier to see they've lost their integrity and simply report their biases. In the last election cycle, many in the main-stream press became mouthpieces for the candidate.

For the most part, business leaders have chosen to stay out of the fray. They are the most capable because they are running successful businesses that increase our GDP and world market share. They could contribute greatly to our leadership, but they are wary of getting involved in the political free for all.

SOME OBSERVATIONS THAT MAY
BE HELPFUL FOR CONTEXT

Let us compare the business process to the political process to understand why one works for all the constituents and the other does not.

1. Business leaders plan for a good ROI. Politicians plan to get re-elected.

2. In business, products are developed that fit customer expectations. The customer writes a check for benefits if satisfied. In politics, programs are developed that pay voters for their vote.

3. A business president sets funding priorities to meet the company's operating plan. The nation's president sets program priorities to please his voter base.

4. In business, managers write operating plans to meet the company president's goals. In politics Congress prepares a legislative agenda to get itself re-elected.

5. Business managers use measurement criteria to ensure results meet or exceed plan. Politicians use measurement criteria to obfuscate results so they are not held accountable.

6. In business, products are shipped on time to customer expectations. Financial reporting provides corrective action to meet or exceed plan within financial constraints. In Congress, projects, and earmarks are attached to bills without being read. There is no financial reporting or progress reporting on meeting the administration's goals.

Clearly if a business is successful then all the constituents are happy. The customers love their purchases, the shareholders get a good ROI, the employees see ever increasing compensation and job satisfaction as they advance through the organization, and the country wins by increasing its GDP.

On the other hand, if a politician is successful by getting re-elected, not all the constituents are happy. Some of the voters are happy, but a majority are not. The special interests are happy if their agenda is met. The campaign staffers are satisfied from a winning campaign. The nation is not satisfied because it considers the government dysfunctional with an approval rating below 30 percent.

There are almost 7 million large business corporations and 18 million small businesses in America today. In the last fifty years, starting in the 1960s with a recognition of the importance of natural competition, most of America's businesses have had to change from a robber baron philosophy in the nineteenth and early twentieth century to a *Compete and Empower* philosophy in order to be successful. Although unions and punitive labor laws in the robber baron days protected specific jobs and working conditions, in today's global marketplace with reformed corporations, these same laws are now counterproductive. In order to be competitive, a business must go down the experience curve without union work stoppages and limits on performance.

During the last one hundred years, politicians and their staffs have taken charge of the government and the citizens, expanded bureaucracy, and criminalized activities that fall under the category of normal business risk. In 2009 they are spending over 30 percent of GDP, which must be funded by the taxpayer, borrowed from foreign investors, or printed by the treasury. During the last one hundred years governments all over the world were sucked in by communism, socialism, or fascism and ran social engineering experiments. In practically every case, they failed and yet today over fifty percent of our politicians still recommend socialist programs instead of self-reliance.

The question we must ask ourselves is this: "Do these politicians keep spending taxpayer money on these social programs because they believe that it's best for the people, or because it gets them re-elected?" In the beginning, one could argue that they care about the people, but after the results are in, is the "caring" pitch a sham to get elected? Today, sadly, it's deemed politically incorrect to question their motives.

Two additional examples come to mind that illuminate the need for leadership change. They are the "Fair Tax" proposal and the "Contract with America."

Most people believe that the current income tax scheme is unworkable, unwieldy, and unfair and is a drag on the economy. Taxpayers must submit paperwork that is almost impossible to complete without making errors. Even the current Treasury secretary could not work it out and had to pay unpaid taxes before he was confirmed. Most taxpayers hire an accountant to help them get it right or as insurance in case the taxpayer is audited. Billions of dollars are wasted on this exercise. Taxpaying does not support self-reliance or small business, and the code is riddled with exceptions to fit one special interest or another. The deck is stacked in favor of re-electing politicians.

WE MUST CHANGE THE TAX CODE

Twenty years ago, a "Fair Tax" movement was started to change the tax system. The concept is to tax consumption through sales tax instead of income. Today this proposal has been refined; it has significant support and is the subject of a book titled, *Fair Tax,* by Neal Boortz and Georgia Congressman John Linder.

Fair Tax Act H.R. 25 was introduced to Congress in 1999 and has had many hearings in committees. It was also supported by Mike Huckabee, a talented presidential candidate in 2008. Even with all this support, it is still stalled in Congress twenty years after its original ideas were generated. Another tax reform program called the "Flat Tax" has also suffered a similar fate.

My purpose here is not to support one proposal over another but to recognize that we must change the tax code to unleash our growth. We need a new tax code, but our government, in defiance of the will of the people, has failed to act.

WE NEED A NEW CONTRACT WITH AMERICA

The "Republican Contract with America" was presented to the people by the Republican Party during the 1994 election season. It was written by Larry Hunter, a lifelong conservative activist, with input from Newt Gingrich, Robert Walker, Richard Armey, Bill Paxon, Tom Delay, John Boehner, and Jim Nussle. Ideas from Ronald Reagan's 1985 State of the Union Address provided helpful guidance.

The results, of this "Republican Contract with America," have been mixed. The original eight tenets were written into ten bills with several elements of the eight tenets being added to other bills. The House brought all ten new bills to the floor. Nine passed the House with the term limit bill failing to pass. Four of the new bills did not get through the Senate, and four were vetoed by the president. Some of the remaining elements in other bills were stalled in the Senate. Some passed after significant modification. Term limits, the most important bill of all, failed to pass because the politicians rigged the game to stay in power.

The elitist attitude of our government is on display over this Contract with America. After it was introduced to the people before the election, the people overwhelmingly voted in a Republican majority in the House and a small Republican majority in the Senate. Clearly based on the results discussed above the *will* of the majority did not get acted on by Congress. It was said that President Clinton called it a Contract *on* America, an elitist thing to say considering the people had spoken with their votes.

The examples discussed above show how difficult it has become for the people to be in charge of the government. The Founding Fathers intended the people to be in charge by giving us the ability to vote the president, vice president, senators, and representatives in or out of office if they did not execute the will of the people. The Founding Fathers also anticipated that the elected politicians would be citizen politicians and not career politicians. By fixing the rules, politicians are getting re-elected for many terms, way beyond the age where they are competent to function. The CEOs of most corporations are required, by policy, to retire in their late sixties.

Newt Gingrich, a historian, prolific writer, and experienced congressman, is very aware of the challenges the people face in order to change the leadership of this country. He has evolved an incremental concept for this change by focusing on solutions to challenges that a majority of voters accept. Even when supported by a majority of both parties, special rules can be invoked by the leadership in House and Senate to make sure the solution does not get a full vote. Newt Gingrich does an excellent job of explaining how to make real change in his 2008 book, *Real Change: From the World that Fails to the World that Works.*

Compete and Empower is my call to action to the American people.

HOW ARE THE PEOPLE AND THE POLITICIANS ORGANIZED?

The Constitution calls out three branches of government with a fourth branch being the states representing the people:

1. The executive branch

2. The legislative branch

3. The judicial branch

4. The fifty states

The relationships and powers between the branches are described by the Founding Fathers in the Constitution.

In a classical sense, most of the government is a staff function to the president, and the people. The House and Senate are staff personnel that make new laws when necessary, approve budgets, and review performance for accountability. The Judicial staff personnel run the courts to enable justice to prevail and monitor judicial decisions for consistency with the Constitution. The Cabinet Departments are staff to the president to make sure his strategic plan is executed. There are seven out of fifteen cabinet departments that have operational responsibilities as well as staff duties.

Approximate Data for the 15 Departments:

	Department	Budget	# Employees	Role
1	Agriculture	$ 95.0 billion	100,000	Staff
2	Commerce	$ 6.8 billion	35,000	Staff
3	Defense	$549.0 billion	3,100,000	Staff & Operations
4	Education	$ 68.6 billion	4,200	Staff
5	Energy	$ 23.0 billion	100,000	Staff
6	Health & Human Services	$700.0 billion	65,000	Staff & Operations
7	Homeland Security	$ 40.0 billion	216,000	Staff & Operations
8	Housing & Urban Develop	$ 40.0 billion	9,000	Staff
9	Interior	$ 16.0 billion	70,000	Staff & Operations
10	Justice	$ 25.0 billion	50,000	Staff & Operations
11	Labor	$ 50.0 billion	15,000	Staff
12	State	$ 35.0 billion	30,000	Staff & Operations
13	Transportation	$ 70.0 billion	55,000	Staff
14	Treasury	$ 13.0 billion	100,000	Staff
15	Veteran Affairs	$ 90.0 billion	235,000	Staff & Operations

What follows are some impressions on the level of spending and organizational accountability through the eyes of the politician, then through the eyes of a business person.

THROUGH THE EYES OF A POLITICIAN

In earlier years, when government was small and taxes were low, a competent, accomplished person might consider running for office to provide a public service. Initially the motive may be to make a contribution and then go back to private enterprise, but intentions change.

The officeholder finds that in order to make a credible contribution, he must participate in the power structure in Washington taking more time to get results. Lo and behold, a career politician is born. All the civilian's good intentions are thrown out the window and replaced with a powerful politician's intention. From this platform, it is often difficult to do the best thing for the people, for America, because it may conflict with career objectives.

Politicians in the legislative branch write our laws, allowing them to tax and spend. While responsibility and power come with bigger budgets and bigger staffs; in government these actions are not tied closely to results. On the other hand, the business person must create great products to satisfy customers, compete in the free market to get growth, control spending to get a high return, and develop an empowering workplace to retain and grow all employees. On top of all these responsibilities, the business and the people must pay for bloated government spending directed by tax and spend politicians.

In summary, a good person enters government where there is a conflict of interest between succeeding as a politician and doing the right thing for the people. The justification for making the government all powerful and in charge of the people is that politicians can say that they are doing the bidding of the people in their district or state. They forget that they rigged the game to stay in power by changing districts and accepting campaign funds from special interests.

Many career politicians, not all, see a large and bloated government that has taken charge over the people. They see an easy opportunity to build a successful lifetime career of increasing personal wealth at the expense of the people. They vote themselves salary increases, hire staffs and limo service to make their lives easier, and establish pensions and medical benefits considerably more valuable than the people's Social Security and Medicare.

THROUGH THE EYES OF A BUSINESS PERSON

A business person looking at the organization sees a lot of similarity with modern business practice. There are literally hundreds of successful conglomerate corporations operating in America today. Their mission and strategies vary from conglomerate to conglomerate depending on the competitive position and differentiation that makes them successful.

The president at corporate headquarters in the business community retains a staff consistent with the services needed to support the businesses. The businesses are usually self-contained with a chief executive or general manager, staff, administrative, and line personnel. The president will most likely use a hands-off management style expecting the independent businesses to operate autonomously and deliver expected results. In some cases, the president may use a more direct management style to supervise a few businesses that need his personal attention. The president is more directly involved in these businesses to ensure that they perform to his expectations.

On further appraisal of the government organization, the business person would associate the 25 million businesses delivering products and services at about $14.2 trillion in 2008 as the autonomous businesses. The seven cabinet departments with operations responsibility would be considered those businesses more directly managed by the president.

Finally he would look at the size and cost of the staff to provide research and checks and balances for a $14.2 trillion level of business and shake his head. He would say to those responsible for such bureaucracy, "Are you crazy?" What do you do? How useful is it? Do you get a good return? Why do you keep adding bloat when the results you deliver get worse?" In the working environment, where the business person expects teamwork and cooperation between staffs, he discovers anarchy. Many of the politicians and leaders are calling the boss names, talking, and leaking information behind his back, broadcasting to America's enemies that the war is lost. Only in government, when politicians reduce the amount of planned spending growth, do they spin it as a painful cut in spending. In other words, a business man would consider the government staff completely dysfunctional.

In summary, any responsible business person would declare the government organization unworkable and recommend wholesale firing, restructuring, and rebuilding to achieve a viable organization that gets things done.

SENSIBLE SOLUTIONS

The "Republican Contract with America" turned out to be an outstanding communication document. Not only did it encourage the voters to act and give control of the House and Senate to the Republicans, it also empowered the politicians to deliver a good portion of the promises. Unfortunately several of the promises were either blocked or stalled by the Senate or the president's veto.

With this powerful precedent, I'd like to propose a new contract, called the **"Citizen's Contract With America."** This new contract should be presented for a vote by referendum at the 2010 elections. If a majority agrees with the solutions, we must find a way to enact the contract into law.

CITIZEN'S CONTRACT WITH AMERICA

As citizens of the United States of America and as business people seeking to unleash the American dream, we propose not to just change government but to transform it into a twenty first-century version of the Constitution and the Founding Fathers' vision. Even importantly, we intend to restore the bonds of trust between the people and their elected representatives.

In this era of official evasion, posturing, and acrimony, we offer a detailed agenda for national renewal, a written commitment with no fine print.

The 2010 election offers the chance, after a century of mismanaged government, to bring to the citizens a referendum to enact the "Citizen's Contract with America." This contract will transform how government works. Such an historic change would spell the end of government that is too big, too intrusive, and too easy with the public's money. It will be the beginning of a new government born in the spirit of the Constitution that respects the values and shares the faith of the American family.

Like Lincoln, our first Republican president, we intend to act "with firmness in the right, as God gives us to see the right": To restore accountability to government, to end the cycle of scandal and disgrace, to make us all proud again of how free, virtuous people govern themselves and share with other nations the concept of *Compete and Empower.*

Within the first one hundred days of the government in 2011, the people expect the following bills to be introduced by the legislative branch. Each is to be given full and open debate, each to be given a clear and fair vote, and each to be passed in accordance with the people's wishes as defined by the referendum vote in November 2010.

The ten acts proposed are as follows:

1. **The Government Reform Act ...** Require the president, senators, representatives, and their appointed political staff to serve only one eight-year term. Having served in any of these capacities, they are not eligible for any other of these positions. Require these same individuals to reside in their own state with their own staff without a Washington office. Expect them to collaborate, debate, and vote by teleconference. An additional benefit of term limits will be an increase in the number of competent citizens who will be able to serve their country. Eliminate all arcane rules that block progress on bills expected to be passed by the citizens. Outside auditors will review all staff functions and government organizations to recommend elimination or budget reductions. Union membership for all government employees will be eliminated. Special retirement and medical programs for all government employees will be eliminated. The employees will be given the opportunity to avail themselves of the same programs that are made available to the general citizen. There should be no special privileges for security and travel

for members of Congress and their staff. They should follow the same security procedures that they set up to keep the citizens safe.

2. **The Compete and Empower Strategy Act ...** Clarify that the highest priority the country has is to increase GDP growth to meet or exceed the strategic plan's market share goal. The president's role in achieving the GDP goal is to support American business. His job is to remove all barriers that interfere with business growth. He must make clear to all his government employees that GDP growth is the country's highest priority. In addition he must encourage all citizens to embrace the principles of GDP growth, learn, grow, and change, and follow the *Compete and Empower* doctrine. Appoint a secretary of Commerce who is an expert in strategic planning from the BCG school. Fund a Strategic Planning Outreach Team (SPOT) with professionals managed by the secretary. Charge the team with the responsibility to facilitate the American Strategic Plan annually, promote *Compete and Empower* around the country and in other nations with a willingness to learn, and set up Strategy Enterprise Zones in nations that sign up for a program.

3. **The Fair Tax and Spend Act ...** Enact the "Fair Tax Proposal" into law during 2011. Require annual federal government budgets to start with a Zero-Based Budget process, meaning no automatic increases in expenses or compensation. Any increase over the prior year is to be based on ROI calculations. All projects and programs must have a plan with expected results. The plans must be monitored and results reported monthly to ensure a

good ROI. All recommended actions from the outside auditors in the first act to be executed. Total federal government spending not to exceed 11 percent of GDP.

4. **The Transform Unions Act ...** Write new labor laws that eliminate the rights of unions. Suggest to all states that they change their labor laws making them "Right to Work" states. Give unions the option of going out of business or becoming trade associations. Terminate all union contracts, and cash out all benefits to members from funds available.

5. **The Embrace Immigrant Act ...** Erect a barrier to limit illegal entry along all borders. The barrier can be physical or based on technology. Direct the Department of Citizenship and Immigration to set a visa goal consistent with the immigration levels called out in the Strategic Plan. There will be only three ways to enter the country legally: a visitor visa for visitors who will return to their home country at expiration, a student visa for students who will return home after their education is complete, unless they are hired by a U.S. business and get a legal entry by the third method, and a green card with most of the privileges of citizenship including the right to become a citizen after five years. Immigration priority will be based on job skills as set by America's businesses. Companies can hire the skills they need when, where, and how they consider appropriate. No more H1 or guest visas, because they do not work and contribute to the illegal immigrant issue. Solve the illegal immigrant challenge by reviewing each case, punishing those who have broken the law, and requiring all to compete with all applicants.

6. **The Protect the People Act ...** As commander in chief, the president has a very highest priority is to protect the people. By Constitution and by law, he has direct control of the Department of Defense and Homeland Security. This act must make it clear that all other politically correct priorities are secondary because the president has taken a solemn oath to keep the people safe. Typical secondary priorities are "Freedom of Speech," "Freedom of Information," "Rules of Engagement," Rules of Interrogation." Information known to be obtained illegally cannot be published by the media. Fully fund the Department of Defense to 5 percent of GDP, and require it to change its mission to execute the strategic plan. Eliminate all barriers that prevent the acquisition of intelligence information to keep us safe domestically and internationally.

7. **The International Empowerment Act ...** This will end our policy of appeasement, diplomacy at any cost, and immoral support of regimes to retain stability over the last thirty years. In its place will be enacted a new policy of pragmatic, moral action to bring about change for a lasting peace. The secretary and the Department will encourage other nations to support *Compete and Empower*. Foreign aid will support SPOT by investing in a nation's businesses and will not be handing out checks to governments. The Foreign Aid Department will be staffed with professional venture fund managers. Diplomacy will make proposals to bring a lasting peace. If not resolved, the other side will expect serious consequences.

8. **The People's Retirement and Health Care Act ...** This act will require the government to inform the citizens that since their inception Social Security and Medicare have been deceptive political schemes. The payments made by citizens into the government and the funds paid out by the government will be reconciled and the remainder placed in an investment fund and managed by professionals. The remainder funds will be owned by the citizens and will be available for their retirement and medical needs. These programs will be removed as mandatory spending programs from government control. In the event there is a shortfall creating hardship on any citizen, the citizen will be able to apply for welfare.

9. **The Government's Enterprise Act ...** The purpose of this change in the law is to take our government out of running businesses it was not intended to run by the Constitution. If the government has control of more than 10 percent of any business, it will be required to sell off these interests with a public offering. The public offerings would be managed by American investment bankers. Businesses likely to be affected are banks, insurance companies, autos, schools, post offices, charities, etc. Private ownership of the schools will emphasize fundamental learning so that American students can compete in a global marketplace. In addition, American children will be encouraged to learn, grow, change, and become self-reliant. teachers will be compensated for performance so that they become proud to be a teacher. The Department of Defense and Homeland Security will continue to be managed by the government, as well as small funds for welfare and charity.

10. The People's Safety Net Act ... Set at 1 percent of
GDP as funding for situations of extreme hardship
where it is appropriate for a modern society to provide
fall back financing when all other avenues have been
exhausted. Two levels seem appropriate: The first level
is when a person needs a helping hand to get back
on his feet. In this case, welfare funding should be
provided as long as the recipient presents a plan of
how and when he will return to being self-reliant. If
the recipient has no experience in such planning and
execution, a welfare counselor can guide him. The
second level is when a person is completely dependent
and needs a source of income to cover living, learning,
and medical costs because of disabilities. This
government charity fund can provide needed help
after family, friends, and local charities have been
approached.

EPILOGUE

"The purpose of life is a life of purpose."
—Robert Byrnes

THE WORLD IS FULL OF PROMISE ...

Keeping the promise has been elusive. Spiritual human beings discovered so much about life when they learned to listen to their creator. With the spirit of life at their back, they can sail any sea, climb any mountain, and travel into space. The accomplishments over 10,000 years are legendary.

We have evolved to be survivors of the fittest, to compete with honor, and to be self-reliant. We have learned about creation, the, origins of space, the physics of the universe, evolution, science, technology, the human body, and the human spirit. The results have been profound. We have invented, developed, and produced products and services that have raised the wealth of the planet for some but not all.

Why has prosperity for all been an elusive dream? Because we have failed to build great societies and nations. What is the secret elixir we are missing? Most people are doing the responsible thing. They are taking care of themselves and their families. Others, who consider themselves leaders, are running around like chickens with their heads cut off creating chaos and noise, heat not light. Have you tried to comprehend breaking news lately in sixty-second sound bites between one hundred and twenty-second ads? Very few people are reflecting on why the world isn't working for most people.

In the beginning of this book, I promised to unravel the mystery of failing societies and propose a solution. I said this book is a wake-up call for America's leaders in government, corporations, and the media and a call to action for U.S. citizens.

As complicated as the world may appear, and as successful as people are as individuals, there is one primary principle that causes our societies and nations to fail: People in power are conquering and oppressing the people. This is in direct conflict with the people's natural survival of the fittest and self-reliant character. The results speak for themselves when 5.5 billion people out of 6.8 billion live in poverty.

The miracle of human life has many significant events with two that were paramount: The creation of the universe and the creation of Homo Sapiens-Sapiens in the creator's image.

The miracle of human civilization, which has yet to live up to its promise, has also two paramount events: the development of the American Constitution in 1777 and the description of natural and strategic competition in 1965.

In Chapters 2, 3, and 4, I described the people's survival instincts and the learned evolution characteristics. In Chapters

5, 6, and 7, I presented the ideas of competition and a possible road to world peace. In Chapters 8 and 9, I laid out an American strategic plan and a call to action with a "Citizen's Contract with America."

I hope you feel I have kept my promise. My dream is that you will come to believe as I do in the greatness of America and that the world has a peaceful future if we follow the *Compete and Empower* doctrine.

ACKNOWLEDGEMENTS

Compete and Empower, with its message of promise for a future filled with peace and prosperity for all mankind, could only have been written by me as a first-time author because of the contributions of so many who filled my life's journey with knowledge, experiences, judgment, intuition, and a passion for life. Let me start my acknowledgement with the most recent contributors first.

THE WORLD OF PUBLISHING

Lynne Lambert deserves my special thanks. She willingly shared her positive opinions on being an author and encouraged me to attend a publishing seminar hosted by Advantage Media. Adam Witty the founder of Advantage Media and the speakers Tom Antion, Wayne Kelly, Wendy Kurtz, Nick Nanton, Greg Stebben, and Jim Ziegler at the conference all inspired me to participate in the publishing business as an author.

Georgia Thomas has been most helpful by introducing me to her friends in publishing Dave Mona recommended Beaver's Pond Press (BPP) as a good group to work with. The BPP team all made valuable contributions to the book as it progressed. My thanks go to Milt Adams (founder), Tom Kerber (president), Dara Beevas (executive editor), Catherine Friend (developmental editor), Jay Monroe (book design and typesetting), April Michelle Davis (proofreading and indexing), Rachel Anderson (publicist), and Amy Cutler, Jordan Wiklund, Heather Kerber who complete the staff.

I am fortunate to be able to count on the support of several distinguished and accomplished colleagues and friends, who have participated in spirited debates on the subject of the book, and have reviewed all or part of the manuscript. I really appreciate their participation. Ty Cobb (distinguished military career-staff to Ronald Reagan), Ty Cobb Jr. (Nevada State Assembly), Steve Metcalf, Elliott Parker, (economics professor, UNR), Bob Goff (founder Sierra Angels), Caleb Cage, Seth Gunsauls, many members of the Sierra Angels. Many thanks go to Bob and Cathy Weise for insightful conversations, including Cathy's idea to require the senators and congressman from each state to reside locally and teleconference with Washington. Robert Hsu, (founder China Strategy), provided significant knowledge on China. His tour of six cities in China, where I met young Chinese talent and tour group members Joe and Lan Shafer, Gloria Hutchinson, Bill Lawson, and Helga Loewvinsohn, was very helpful. Business associates who always give me good ideas and make time for me when I call are: Fred Lipsig, the late Mike Burd, Doug Hajjar, and Bill Thurston. Members of Thunder Canyon Country Club and people living nearby have been helpful. Roger and Gayle Block-Owners and Mike McGee convinced me to read Zinn's book. Stan and Shyrl

Bailey contributed Clousen's book, Len Semas (publisher Sierra Sage), Dave Semas (CEO Metalast), Larry Goodnight, Bill Coplin, Erez Borowski, Roger Williams, Don Conway, and Sue Knight. Other contributors are Bill Peter, Dr. Lyons, Dr. Ressler and Dr. Hackshaw. A special thank you goes to Jerry Harrison, Bill Nicholson, and Mike Murnin—all successful executives for reviewing the manuscript.

FAMILY AND FAMILY FRIENDS

...continue to debate the issues and egg me on to improvement. My eldest son, Mark, has been invaluable. Somehow he finds time from his busy schedule to lead our family and advise me on ways to make sure we have a successful publication launch. His review of the manuscript brought out several areas for improvement. Jen, Mark's wife, and their children, Matthew and Megan, along with Jen's parents, Ken and Toni Harkness, contribute to my well being enabling me to be creative. Thanks Jen. Stephen, my other son, and his family, Ann Marie, Casey, Sean, Ryan, and Claire, along with Joe and Dolores Casey, are always supportive. They live nearby and are a source of joy and encouragement always. Thanks Ann Marie. Janet Holtby, Paul Holtby and Diane Cooper, along with the late Pete Holtby, have been instrumental in contributing to an Internet enterprise to promote and brand the book. The Holtby's have also been a strong support for the Sear family for forty-four years. Carol Merriam participated in developing a title for the book. Her daughter Joni Simms suggested I read *Rich Dad Poor Dad* several years ago, which contributed to ideas on wealth accumulation. David Sear, my brother meets with me from time to time. The spirited debates have been a big help. David's wife, Pat, and their daughter, Lisa, and son, Jon, have always been supportive at family gatherings.

THE FORMATIVE YEARS

Merle, the love of my life for thirty-eight years, passed away in 1990 after a two-year fight with cancer. Merle's contributions to the man I am today are so significant that I could not do it justice in this limited section. Suffice it to say, she was with me every step of the way. As partners and lovers, we learned, grew, and changed every day. It was a journey of growth with plenty of pain and pleasure to go around. I do not grieve for what could have been but rejoice often in the gift of love and partnership with Merle that was made possible by our Creator. Members of Merle's family always encouraged us. Her parents, Jim and Pat, brother, Derek, and family, and Merle's grandparents, were helpful in so many ways.

I would like to acknowledge the contribution from so many: The teachers at the Emanuel School, Battersea, London England, many school boy friend's there, including Richard Dudley, Brian Price, Alan Twort, Chris Banwell, Michael Blow, and Peter Small; my supervisor, at Shell Petroleum, who suggested Outward Bound, The instructors and participants in my group at Outward Bound; my senior officers in the RAF who taught me radar technology and my good friend John Glenny; my brother, Roger, and family and my cousins who all live in England today; Bruce Hicks my boss at EMP Electric, my first technical job after leaving the RAF; my friend, John Ryder, who taught me so much at Decca Radar; my friends, Maureen and Vic Long and family, who have been our family friends for fifty-five years; the vice president of Human Resources from Univac, who offered me the engineering position in the research department in 1960; the many friends at Univac who emigrated from the UK in the summer of 1960; Drexel University staff and professors who qualified me for an MSEE program and contributed to my analytical knowledge; Bob Parks, who offered me a promotion to become a scientist at Martin Marietta in Maryland in 1962; Don Fuller (senior vice president), Tom Taggart (president and the vice president of finance) who mentored me at Redcor, Canoga Park, California from 1966 to 1969.

I always remember how much I owe my parents, Jack and Elizabeth, who encouraged me all the time to be the best that I can be.

Thank you all.

APPENDIX

Please give me your feedback by writing your comments on my blog at www.briansbusinessblog.com

WHAT TO DO NEXT

It is not going to be easy to make the changes I am proposing. The people in power will not give it up easily even though it's what's best for America. I believe in the American people who have the courage to get it done.

There are several grassroot movements established along with individual Web sites enabling citizens to communicate with their politicians. A few are listed here for your action to support.

- American Solutions, Newt Gingrich, www.americansolutions.com

- Tea Party Groups, http://teapartyexpress.org http://arizonateaparty.com

http://freedomswings.wordpress.com
www.reteaparty.com

- Dick Morris, www.dickmorris.com

- Glen Beck, www.glennbeck.com

- Sean Hannity, www.hannity.com

- Rush Limbaugh, www.rushlimbaugh.com

1994 REPUBLICAN CONTRACT WITH AMERICA

*As Republican members of the House of Representatives
and as citizens seeking to join that body, we propose not just to
change its policies, but, even more important, to restore the bonds
of trust between the people and their elected representatives.*

That is why, in this era of official evasion and posturing, we offer instead a detailed agenda for national renewal, a written commitment with no fine print.

This year's election, 1994, offers the chance, after four decades of one-party control, to bring to the House a new majority that will transform the way Congress works. That historic change would be the end of government that is too big, too intrusive, and too easy with the public's money. It can be the beginning of a Congress that respects the values and shares the faith of the American family.

Like Lincoln, our first Republican president, we intend to act "with firmness in the right, as God gives us to see the right." To restore accountability to Congress. To end its cycle of scandal and disgrace. To make us all proud again of the way free people govern themselves.

On the first day of the 104th Congress, the new Republican majority will immediately pass the following major reforms aimed at restoring the faith and trust of the American people in their government:

> **FIRST**, require all laws that apply to the rest of the country also apply equally to the Congress;

> **SECOND**, select a major, independent auditing firm to conduct a comprehensive audit of Congress for waste, fraud, or abuse;

THIRD, cut the number of House committees, and cut committee staff by one-third;

FOURTH, limit the terms of all committee chairs;

FIFTH, ban the casting of proxy votes in committee;

SIXTH, require committee meetings to be open to the public;

SEVENTH, require a three-fifths majority vote to pass a tax increase;

EIGHTH, guarantee an honest accounting of our federal budget by implementing zero base-line budgeting.

Thereafter, within the first one hundred days of the 104th Congress, we shall bring to the House Floor the following bills, each to be given full and open debate, each to be given a clear and fair vote, and each to be immediately available this day for public inspection and scrutiny.

1. **THE FISCAL RESPONSIBILITY ACT:** A balanced budget/tax limitation amendment and a legislative line-item veto to restore fiscal responsibility to an out-of-control Congress, requiring them to live under the same budget constraints as families and businesses.

2. **THE TAKING BACK OUR STREETS ACT:** An anti-crime package including stronger truth-in sentencing, "good faith" exclusionary rule exemptions, effective death penalty provisions, and cuts in social spending from this summer's "crime" bill to fund prison construction and additional law enforcement to keep people secure in their neighborhoods and kids safe in their schools.

3. **THE PERSONAL RESPONSIBILITY ACT:**
    Discourage illegitimacy and teen pregnancy by prohibiting
    welfare to minor mothers and denying increased Aid to
    Families with Dependent Children for additional children
    while on welfare, cut spending for welfare programs,
    and enact a tough two-years-and-out provision with
    work requirements to promote individual responsibility.

4. **THE FAMILY REINFORCEMENT ACT:** Child
    support enforcement, tax incentives for adoption,
    strengthening rights of parents in their children's
    education, stronger child pornography laws, and an
    elderly dependent care tax credit to reinforce the
    central role of families in American society.

5. **THE AMERICAN DREAM RESTORATION
    ACT:** A $500 per child tax credit, begin repeal of the
    marriage tax penalty, and creation of American dream
    Savings Accounts to provide middle-class tax relief.

6. **THE NATIONAL SECURITY RESTORATION
    ACT:** No U.S. troops under UN command and
    restoration of the essential parts of our national
    security funding to strengthen our national defense
    and maintain our credibility around the world.

7. **THE SENIOR CITIZENS FAIRNESS ACT:** Raise
    the Social Security earnings limit which currently
    forces seniors out of the workforce, repeal the 1993
    tax hikes on Social Security benefits, and provide tax
    incentives for private long-term care insurance to let
    older Americans keep more of what they have earned
    over the years.

8. **THE JOB CREATION AND WAGE ENHANCEMENT ACT:** Small business incentives, capital gains cut and indexation, neutral cost recovery, risk assessment/cost-benefit analysis, strengthening the Regulatory Flexibility Act, and unfunded mandate reform to create jobs and raise worker wages.

9. **THE COMMONSENSE LEGAL REFORM ACT:** "Loser pays" laws, reasonable limits on punitive damages, and reform of product liability laws to stem the endless tide of litigation.

10. **THE CITIZEN LEGISLATURE ACT:** A first-ever vote on term limits to replace career politicians with citizen legislators.

Further, we will instruct the House Budget Committee to report to the floor and we will work to enact additional budget savings, beyond the budget cuts specifically included in the legislation described above, to ensure that the federal budget deficit will be less than it would have been without the enactment of these bills.

Respecting the judgment of our fellow citizens as we seek their mandate for reform, we hereby pledge our names to this Contract with America.

NOTES AND REFERENCES

Boortz, Neal, and John Linder. *FairTax: The Truth: Answering the Critics*. New York: Harper Paperbacks, 2008.

BrainyQuote. Byrne, Robert. http://www.brainyquote.com/quotes/quotes/r/robertbyrn101054.html.

Bruno, Andorra. "Immigration: Policy Considerations Related to Guest Worker Programs." http://trac.syr.edu/immigration/library/P333.pdf.

Businessballs. "Maslow's Hierarchy of Needs." http://www.businessballs.com/maslow.htm.

Clark, Gregory. *A Farewell to Alms: A Brief Economic History of the World*. Princeton, NJ: Princeton University Press, 2008.

Clouser, Roy A. "Genesis on the Origin of the Human Race." *Perspectives on Science and Christian Faith* 43 (March 1991): 2–13.

Daily, Gretchen C., and Paul R. Ehrlich. "Population, Sustainability, and Earth's Carrying Capacity." *BioScience* (November 1, 1992).

Deming, W. Edwards. "Deming's 14 Point Plan for TQM." http://www.1000advices.com/guru/quality_tqm_14points_deming.html.

EarthTrends. "Population Data." http://earthtrends.wri.org.

Extreme Science. "How Old is the Earth?" http://www.extremescience.com/earth.htm.

Faiola, Anthony. "The End of American Capitalism?" *Washington Post* (October 10, 2008). http://www.washingtonpost.com/wp-dyn/content/article/2008/10/09/AR2008100903425.html.

Gingrich, Newt. *Real Change from the World that Fails to the World that Works.* Old Saybrook, CT: Tantor Media Inc., 2008.

GovSpot. "Unions." http://www.govspot.com/govemployees/unions.htm.

Greenspan, Alan. *The Age of Turbulence: Adventures in a New World.* New York: Penguin, 2008.

Heritage Foundation. "The. Social Security Spending Soon to Rise Rapidly." http://www.heritage.org/research/features/budgetchartbook/social-security-spending-soon-to-rise-rapidly.aspx.

Immigration Direct. "Green Cards." http://www.immigrationdirect.com/greencard/index.jsp?gclid=CJToz6-uypwCFRlcagodXxpVmg.

Kaiser Family Foundation. "Medicare Spending and Financing Fact Sheet." http://www.kff.org/medicare/7305.cfm.

Maddison, Angus. *Contours of the World Economy, 1–2030 AD: Essays on Macro-Economic History.* Mario Rostoni Library, Universita Carlo Cattaneo, 2009.

Malthus, Thomas R. *An Essay on the Principle of Population.* Mineola, NY: Dover Publications, 2007.

Marrus, Stephanie K. *Building the Strategic Plan: Find, Analyze, and Present the Right Information.* Malabar, FL: Krieger Publishing Company, 1994.

Michigan Live. "A Brief History of General Motors Corp." http://www.mlive.com/business/index.ssf/2008/09/a_brief_history_of_general_mot.html.

Moore, Geoffrey A. *Crossing the Chasm.* New York: Harper Paperbacks, 2002.

Morris, Dick, and Eileen McGann. *Catastrophe.* New York: Harper, 2009.

Outward Bound Trust, The. "Outward Bound Schools in the UK." http://www.theoutwardboundtrust.org.uk/indexnew.html.

Rand, Ayn. *Atlas Shrugged.* New York: Plume, 1999.

Reagan 2020. "Ronald Reagan, State of the Union Address, 1986." http://reagan2020.us/speeches/state_of_the_union_1986.asp.

Sandy, Leo R., and Ray Perkins Jr. "The Nature of Peace and Its Implications for Peace Education." http://www.uio.no/studier/emner/jus/jus/.../2A%20-%20Reading.doc.

Skousen, W. Cleon. *The 5000 Year Leap: A Miracle that Changed the World.* Malta, ID: National Center for Constitutional Studies, 1981.

Stern, Carl. *The Boston Consulting Group on Strategy: Classic Concepts and New Perspectives.* Hoboken, NJ: Wiley, 2006.

United Nations. "Charter of the United Nations." http://www.un.org/en/documents/charter/chapter4.shtml.

U.S. Census Bureau. "Statistics of U.S. Businesses." http://www.census.gov/econ/susb.

U.S. Department of Health and Human Services. "The 2009 HHS Poverty Guidelines." http://aspe.hhs.gov/poverty/09poverty.shtml.

U.S. Department of Labor. "Employment & Unemployment Statistics." http://www.dol.gov/dol/topic/statistics/employment.htm.

U.S. Department of Labor. "Bureau of Labor Statistics." Productivity and Costs, Second Quarter 2009, Revised. http://www.bls.gov/news.release/prod2.nr0.htm.

U.S. General Services Administration's Office of Citizen Services and Communications. "GDP Data." http://www.usa.gov.

USGovernmentSpending. "Federal Budgeted Government Spending." http://www.usgovernmentspending.com/fed_overall_federal_spending_chart_09_F.html.

U.S. House of Representatives. "Republican Contract with America." http://www.house.gov/house/Contract/CONTRACT.html.

U.S. State Department. "Strategic Plan." http://www.state.gov/documents/organization/86291.pdf.

Wiker, Benjamin, and William Dembski. *Moral Darwinism: How We Became Hedonists*. Downers Grove, IL: InterVarsity Press, 2002.

Wikipedia. "BRIC." http://en.wikipedia.org/wiki/BRIC.

Wikipedia. "Carlos Santana." http://en.wikipedia.org/wiki/Carlos_Santana.

Wikipedia. "Community Re-Investment Act." http://en.wikipedia.org/wiki/Community_Reinvestment_Act.

Wikipedia. "Declaration of Independence." http://en.wikipedia.org/wiki/Declaration_of_independence.

Wikipedia. "Emanuel School." http://en.wikipedia.org/wiki/Emanuel_School.

Wikipedia. "Experience curve effects." http://en.wikipedia.org/wiki/Experience_curve_effects.

Wikipedia. "First Inauguration of Ronald Reagan." http://en.wikipedia.org/wiki/First_Inaugural_address_of_Ronald_Reagan.

Wikipedia. "H-1B Visa." http://en.wikipedia.org/wiki/H-1B_visa.

Wikipedia. "Homo Sapiens (disambiguation)." http://en.wikipedia.org/wiki/Homo_sapiens_(disambiguation).

Wikipedia. "Hugo Chávez." http://en.wikipedia.org/wiki/Hugo_Chávez.

Wikipedia. "Immigration and Nationality Act of 1965." http://en.wikipedia.org/wiki/Immigration_and_Nationality_Act_of_1965.

Wikipedia. "Immigration to the United States." http://en.wikipedia.org/wiki/Immigration_to_the_United_States.

Wikipedia. "Karl Marx." http://en.wikipedia.org/wiki/Karl_Marx.

Wikipedia. "League of Nations." http://en.wikipedia.org/wiki/League_of_Nations.

Wikipedia. "Mein Kampf." http://en.wikipedia.org/wiki/Mein_Kampf.

Wikipedia. "Military budget of the United States." http://en.wikipedia.org/wiki/Military_budget_of_the_United_States.

Wikipedia. "Robert Higgs." http://en.wikipedia.org/wiki/Robert_Higgs.

Wikipedia. "Troubled Asset Relief Program." http://en.wikipedia.org/wiki/Troubled_Asset_Relief_Program.

Wikipedia. "United Nations." http://en.wikipedia.org/wiki/United_Nations.

Wikipedia. "United States Constitution." http://en.wikipedia.org/wiki/U.S._Constitution.

"Who Pays for Cap and Trade?" *Wall Street Journal* (March 9, 2009). http://online.wsj.com/article/SB123655590609066021.html.

Woods, Thomas E., Jr., and Ron Paul. *Meltdown: A Free-Market Look at Why the Stock Market Collapsed, the Economy Tanked, and Government Bailouts Will Make Things Worse.* Washington, DC: Regnery Press, 2009.

Zinn, Howard, Mike Konopacki, and Paul Buhle. *A People's History of American Empire.* New York: Metropolitan Books, 2008.

INDEX

ABOUT THE AUTHOR

Early stage new ventures, growth companies in emerging markets, and real estate opportunities keep Brian Sear busy and energized. He is a member of the Sierra Angels and is president of VenRaD LLC, a venture research and development consultancy in Washoe Valley, Nevada, a small town just outside Reno.

Before starting VenRaD LLC in 1985, Sear had a successful career in high technology. He was recruited in London, England to join the Univac research team working on its first semiconductor computer. This began a productive period developing and patenting new technology and publishing the results. During the 1960s and 1970s Sear published many articles in prestigious journals and went on speaking tours to promote novel ideas about computers and instrumentation.

Sear still meets with clients, advising CEOs, directors, and investors on steps they should take to grow business despite the tough economy. No matter what the industry, he applies the fundamental principles of natural competition to superior strategy development. Working with the Board, CEO, and management team, Sear prepares a strategic framework that represents the thinking and judgment of top management about the future of the company. This due diligence provides both parties with a path to proceed if the venture is promising.

Sear has plenty of experience in that regard. Between 1969 and the present, he has started up several multimillion dollar companies that achieved good results. He has been the leader in companies both private and public. In recent years, his focus shifted to becoming an author and developing an Internet enterprise.

"While spending time in China back in 2007, I discovered a nation with strategic clarity and intent to grow its people out of poverty by making China's growth of gross domestic product its highest priority. I admired what they were doing," says Sear. "I came home to America, the greatest democracy the world has ever known because of its citizens and Constitution and realized our Washington leaders, mired in political correctness, are failing our citizens, and do not deserve to lead this capable country of ours. If not redirected, they will diminish this great nation."

Sear is now on a mission to help get America back on the road to prosperity and wealth. He says we need to "Enact a new Citizen's Contract with America" that eliminates career politicians and replaces them with citizen politicians—public servants whose highest ideal is to serve the people.

"Corporate America needs to make changes as well," says Sear. "Rather than collaborating with and appeasing the